NATIVE CHIEFS AND FAMOUS MÉTIS

AMAZING STORIES

NATIVE CHIEFS AND FAMOUS MÉTIS

Leadership and Bravery in the Canadian West

NATIVE/HISTORY

by Holly Quan

To Sue, who pursues her own vision of Spirit

PUBLISHED BY ALTITUDE PUBLISHING CANADA LTD.
1500 Railway Avenue, Canmore, Alberta T1W 1P6
www.altitudepublishing.com
1-800-957-6888

Extreme care has been taken to ensure that all information presented in
this book is accurate and up to date. Neither the author nor the
publisher can be held responsible for any errors.

Publisher	Stephen Hutchings
Associate Publisher	Kara Turner
Editor	Debbie Elicksen
Digital photo colouring & map	Scott Manktelow

We acknowledge the financial support of the Government
of Canada through the Book Publishing Industry Development
Program (BPIDP) for our publishing activities.

Altitude GreenTree Program
Altitude Publishing will plant twice as many trees as were used
in the manufacturing of this product.

National Library of Canada Cataloguing in Publication Data

Quan, Holly
Native chiefs & famous Métis / Holly Quan.

(Amazing stories)
Includes bibliographical references.
ISBN 1-55153-965-9

1. Indians of North America--Prairie Provinces--Kings and rulers--
Biography. 2. Métis--Prairie Provinces--Biography.
I. Title. II. Series: Amazing stories (Canmore, Alta.)

E89.Q35 2003   971.2'00497'00922   C2003-905474-8

An application for the trademark for Amazing Stories™
has been made and the registered trademark is pending.

Printed and bound in Canada by Friesens
2 4 6 8 9 7 5 3

Cover: Chief Crowfoot of the Blackfoot
(Reproduced with permission from the Glenbow Archives)

Contents

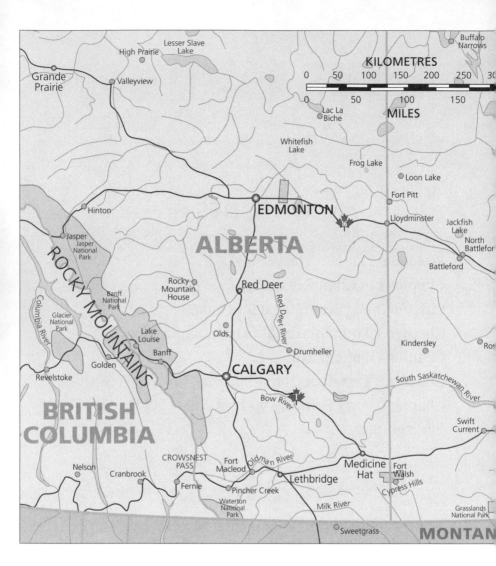

Author's Note

This book is a different kind of adventure story. The stories here are true, though I have embellished them with my own imagination and interpretations of what may have been going through the hearts and minds of the people involved. They are tales of bravery and courage, of decisive action in times of terrible conflict. They are the stories of heroes, both leaders and ordinary men, who found themselves

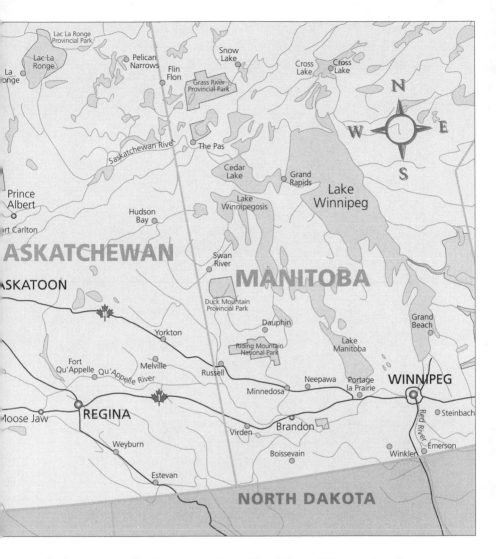

playing major roles in western Canadian history. What makes these
stories different is the ring of sadness and loss.

The amazing stories in this book are no less amazing because
they are tragic. These men and their great deeds have left their mark
on Native culture and on the history of the West. They are inspiring
stories, even though many end in sorrow, defeat, even death. They
are the stories of great and wise men, and I'm proud to share them
with you.

Prologue

The Iron Stone had always been there...embedded in a hillside. To the Blackfoot and Cree of the western plains, the Iron Stone was the embodiment of powerful spirits, a source of strength, power, protection, and luck. In spring, people travelled great distances to the Iron Stone. They burned sweetgrass. They sang songs of celebration. They asked the stone for good hunting.

In later times, geologists would say the Iron Stone was a meteorite that landed near the present-day town of Killam, Alberta. The Iron Stone weighed about 200 kilograms, one of the largest meteorites ever found in Canada.

To the Reverend George McDougall, the Iron Stone was a pagan symbol. With considerable effort in the early spring of 1866, he had the stone dug from its resting place, loaded onto a wagon, and carted to Victoria mission, east of Edmonton. But that wasn't the end of the stone's journey. McDougall sent it by boat down the North Saskatchewan River to Fort Garry and on to Toronto, to be proudly displayed on the lawn of the Methodist college, where he was trained — a trophy of his struggle to tame the people of the western plains.

That spring, when the Cree and Blackfoot came again to visit the Iron Stone, they were shocked to discover an enormous tragedy: their source of protection was gone. Their link with the buffalo spirits, their defence against evil and disasters, had mysteriously vanished. The elders predicted war, disease, and starvation.

All their predictions came true.

Chapter 1
A Changing World

The First Nations and Métis of the West had a long tradition that honoured courage. Courage in battle when faced with fierce and relentless enemies. Courage to hunt buffalo, grizzlies, elk, eagles, bighorn sheep, and more. Courage to face the intense heat of a summer drought or the bone-chilling cold of a prairie blizzard. Courage to seek visions through fasting, painful rites of passage, and courage to interpret and act upon those visions. And, more than anything, courage to confront sweeping changes that would shake their culture and traditional ways to the very core.

These are the amazing stories of five remarkable

men, each of whom played a major part in the clash of cultures that occurred in the Canadian West. Three of these men — Crowfoot, Big Bear, and Poundmaker — were aboriginal, while the other two, Jerry Potts and Peter Erasmus, were Métis. All were revered, respected, and sometimes feared for their leadership, insight, and courage.

Despite vast distances and different backgrounds, the lives of these five men intertwined. Some of them met face to face — occasionally as adversaries — but even if they didn't meet, their names were certainly known to one another. Against a backdrop of difficult times that included starvation, epidemics, and war, these five men stood tall in their efforts to bridge two cultures.

The Buffalo Days

The First Nations of the western plains — a region known as the North West Territory, or simply North West — were nomadic peoples, roaming large territories in search of food. The Blackfoot, Peigan, Blood, and Cree had a centuries-old culture that revolved around the buffalo (also called bison), which provided food, clothing, shelter, tools, and implements, even toys and games. Buffalo were also the centre of the Native peoples' spiritual beliefs, their annual movements, and migrations.

A Changing World

The Blackfoot were supreme rulers between the Bow and the Oldman rivers. To the south, well into what is now Montana, lived the Peigan. To the east were the Blood; to the northwest were the Sarcee. These nations made up the Blackfoot Confederacy, the most powerful alliance on the plains.

North and east of Blackfoot country was the territory of the Plains Cree, whose lands included the North Saskatchewan River. The aptly named Battle River formed a rough dividing line between Blackfoot and Cree. In the woodlands to the north of the Plains Cree were the Woods Cree, Chippewa, and Ojibwa. On the Plains Crees' eastern flank lived the Assiniboine. Some time in the 1800s, a splinter group of Assiniboine, the Stoneys, left the valley of the Qu'Appelle River and travelled west to establish themselves along the Bow River near present-day Banff, on the fringes of Blackfoot territory.

In the time before horses, there were many techniques for hunting buffalo. Occasionally, herds could be stampeded over high cliffs or lured into pounds (corrals) made from skins, brush, and logs. When horses were introduced to the northern plains in the late 1700s, a new hunting method soon developed. Mounted hunters could ride right along side a galloping buffalo so the rider could shoot the animal as it ran. "Buffalo runners"

— horses trained to run beside a stampeding bison — became prized possessions, and the Blackfoot were the plains' greatest horsemen.

Horses brought many other changes to First Nations of the plains. They made travel much easier and were a sign of wealth. Stealing horses became an act of bravery by which young men could prove themselves. Raiding parties frequently stole horses from enemy bands.

War between nations was a fact of life. It was so ingrained in aboriginal cultures that most First Nations bands had two leaders: a chief who led the band during peaceful times and a war chief who took control when the band was under attack. The most frequent and fearsome attacks were between the Blackfoot and the Cree nations, who were bitter enemies. These two nations sparred constantly. Young warriors stole horses, murdered enemies, and kidnapped women and children as prisoners and slaves.

So it was for countless generations. Then came the fur traders.

Winds of Change

According to a Royal Charter dated 1670, the Hudson's Bay Company (HBC) was granted exclusive rights to an enormous tract of land from the Rocky Mountains to

A Changing World

Hudson Bay. Europeans gradually penetrated the Native lands in search of furs. The newcomers built isolated trading posts throughout the West, especially in the northern woodlands, where beaver, mink, muskrat, and other fur-bearing animals were plentiful. The HBC had control of this vast territory until 1869, when the company sold their land holdings to the brand-new Dominion of Canada. Just two years earlier, in 1867, the British North America Act had established Canada as a country, though it was little more than a collection of tiny farms and far-flung communities in the Great Lakes and Maritimes regions, far to the east of the great plains and northwestern woodlands.

The traders took Native wives and their children became a nation in their own right: the Métis Nation. Renowned scouts and buffalo hunters, the Métis' main settlements were along the Red River in the Fort Garry region (now Winnipeg) and in central Saskatchewan.

The 49th parallel — to Native peoples, the Medicine Line — was established in 1849 as the division between American and British territories. The vast and unmapped lands north of the line continued to be of great interest to the Americans, who knew that Britain had only the slimmest of footholds. In 1857, the British government sent a team of explorers and scientists under Captain John Palliser, to assess the region for mineral and other resources, and the potential for settlement. Missionaries also entered the country, building missions, churches, and schools.

Many changes came with the arrival of Europeans. The newcomers brought diseases, to which the Native peoples of the West had never been exposed. The worst of these was smallpox, but there were others such as measles, whooping cough, scarlet fever, and more.

Most importantly, Native peoples were no longer the only hunters on the plains. Europeans, Americans, and Métis also competed for buffalo. And so the great bison slaughter began. Animals were killed by the thousands, often only for their tongues. As the herds dwindled, the cultural and economic underpinning of traditional aboriginal ways came undone. By the 1870s, Native peoples began to starve. They were forced to move south into hostile country in search of food.

Although the HBC set up many fur-trading posts along the North Saskatchewan River, including Battleford, Fort Carlton, Fort Pitt, and Fort Edmonton, attempts to set up trade agreements with the fierce, proud Blackfoot failed. But traders of a different kind eventually found favour with the Blackfoot: whisky traders.

In 1869, when the HBC sold their lands to the Canadian government, the company traders lost whatever influence and authority they had in the West. Into this vacuum came Americans, bringing rotgut whisky from Montana to trade with Native peoples north of the Medicine Line. Outlaw whisky traders set up their well-fortified posts in hidden coulees and dispensed liquor in return for buffalo robes, horses, guns, moccasins, women — anything. What little law and order that had existed on the plains quickly disintegrated. In 1871, there were 88 alcohol-related murders among the Blackfoot alone.

A People Under Siege

Into this fray of war, disease, hunger, and the lawless, freewheeling whisky trade marched the North West Mounted Police (NWMP). In 1874, the red-coated police force arrived on the plains to eradicate the whisky trade. Initially, the police won the respect of Native peoples for their fair and even-handed treatment of anyone who broke the law, but in later years, that trust would be broken.

Aside from rooting out whisky traders, the NWMP had another mission: to make the North West Territories safe for settlement. The new government of Canada wanted to firmly establish its authority over the West. The best way to do that was to build farms, factories, mills, mines, and towns across the plains. Such a plan would require a railway, of course. And such a plan left no room for the wandering ways of the First Nations.

So in 1876 and 1877, the Dominion government sent representatives to make treaties, first with the Cree, then with the Blackfoot. Thinly disguised as offers to protect aboriginal peoples from starvation, by teaching them farming and other new skills, the treaties actually forced Native peoples to surrender their lands and live within the confines of reserves — at the mercy of government rations and domination.

Nonetheless, Native peoples welcomed the treaties. Confused and suffering from disease, the ravages of whisky, and starvation, they were bewildered and angry. Most of all, they were uncertain about their future and how to deal with the Dominion government. There was great pressure on the elders and chiefs to sign the treaties, to obtain rations and treaty payments.

But for the Cree and Blackfoot peoples, the treaties brought no relief. Buffalo herds continued to wane, bringing tremendous hardship to the western plains. The swift and sudden disappearance of the buffalo left no time for Native peoples to settle on their treaty lands and learn how to be farmers and carpenters. Instead, the people descended further into poverty.

The Métis nation, too, had its quarrels with the government of Canada. Their leader, Louis Riel, mounted two armed uprisings. In 1871, Riel was defeated and fled into Montana, where he tried to build support for his cause. In 1885, the second Métis rebellion also brought the grievances of the Blackfoot and Cree peoples to a head.

These turbulent times form the setting for the stories of five amazing men, each of whom came to play a role in the changing of the West from the buffalo days to the rebellion of 1885 and beyond.

Chapter 2
Big Bear
(Mistahimusqua)

B ig Bear was a small man with a big heart. Through his mystic visions, he developed a deep fear for the survival of the Plains Cree. He steadfastly stood up for the rights of his people at tremendous personal cost.

Mistahimusqua — Big Bear — was born about 1825 into a band of Plains Cree who lived in the area of Jackfish Lake, north of today's city of North Battleford, Saskatchewan. He was the son of Black Powder, a Cree chief. His mother may have been from the Ojibwa nation.

Black Powder's band lived on the northern edge of the buffalo range, partly on the plains, partly in the woods. In the summer, the band ventured onto the open prairie to hunt buffalo. In winter, they hunted deer, moose, even beaver in the woodlands and lakes to the north. The closest HBC outposts were Fort Carlton and Fort Pitt, each about 130 kilometres away, one to the east, the other west.

In 1837, when Big Bear was 12 years old, he caught smallpox but he survived. Though his face was deeply scarred by the disease, his countenance was wise and open. He loved to laugh and tell stories. He was also a private person, meditative, and spiritual in nature.

Big Bear spent his youth in the free-roaming days, when horse stealing raids and war parties against enemy tribes were opportunities for a young man to prove himself. As son of a chief, Big Bear was expected to be even more bold and fearless than his companions. These traits he revealed, but the Cree also respected Big Bear for another reason: his amazing visions.

Big Bear's Visions
Throughout his life, Big Bear used his dreams and visions to guide his decisions and actions. Three of his visions had special significance.

The first of these came to him while recovering from smallpox. In this disturbing vision, Big Bear foresaw the coming of European settlers, mass suffering of his people, and the surrender of Native lands. Merely a boy at the time, Big Bear could hardly give credit to this vision. After all, buffalo were plentiful, the Cree ruled a large territory, tormented their Blackfoot enemies, and there were only a handful of traders, trappers, and other Europeans throughout the North West. How could such a thing come to pass as settlers overrunning Cree lands?

In the second vision, a spirit offered Big Bear the opportunity for great wealth as the owner of many horses, but first he would have to succeed in a test. The spirit took Big Bear to a cave filled with fine horses and instructed him to walk through the milling herd to capture the single horse he would find in the centre. In his dream, Big Bear boldly strode into the herd until he encountered a stallion that reared up, flailing his front hooves. The young chief moved to protect himself. Instantly, the cave was empty, except for the spirit who told Big Bear that because of his foolish action, he would never be wealthy in horses. Big Bear interpreted this dream to mean that even when he was successful in horse stealing raids, he should keep only one or two, and give the other horses away — which he always did. Throughout his life, Big Bear was known for his generosity.

As a young man seeking guidance through a vision, Big Bear went alone to a sacred place on the Red Deer River to fast and meditate. During his vision quest, Big

Bear had the most powerful of his three famous visions, which in turn led to an incident that has become a legend among the Cree.

A bear spirit appeared and offered lifelong protection if Big Bear would go back to his camp and prepare a medicine bundle according to the bear spirit's direction. Thereafter, the Plains Cree people held Big Bear in great reverence because it was rare and exceptional for a bear spirit to honour a young person in this way.

Some time afterward, Black Powder's band was camped far to the southwest of their usual home territory. Black Powder took several hunters in search of bison, leaving young men, including Big Bear, in charge of the camp. In the afternoon, Big Bear left the camp and ventured out to look for bison himself. He rode a long way and was alone on the prairie.

As he rode up a ridge, he heard horses behind him. Turning, to his horror, he saw Blackfoot warriors galloping after him. He knew that if the fighters caught him, they would kill him, then go looking for the rest of his band and family. Big Bear rode over the ridge and into a coulee choked with willow brush. He jumped from his horse's back and rolled under some bushes to hide. The Blackfoot men came into the coulee and thoroughly searched for their Cree quarry. Incredibly, they failed to find him. Big Bear waited a long time, finally daring to emerge and walk back to camp. When he told his story, the band was awestruck. Clearly, Big Bear had the power to become invisible to his enemies, a direct benefit of his bear spirit protector.

In his 20s, Big Bear married an Ojibwa woman, with whom he had several children. In later years, one of his sons, Imasees (Bad Child), would cause much trouble and heartache to Big Bear.

Black Powder died in the 1860s when Big Bear was about 40 years old, well advanced in years and wisdom. Having proved himself in battle and having a reputation as a mystic, due to his many visions and his powerful bear spirit protector, Big Bear took over his father's position as chief. At the time, his band consisted of about 100 people, but he would become a leader and spokesman for the entire Cree nation.

Treaty Six: Seeking a Better Deal
In the fall of 1875, the Reverend George McDougall came to Big Bear's camp with gifts of tobacco and a message: the Dominion government wanted to gather all the Cree peoples and make a treaty with them. There would be two treaty meetings, one at Fort Carlton (near the confluence of the North and South Saskatchewan rivers, in the vicinity of the present-day city of Prince Albert, Saskatchewan) the other at Fort Pitt (east of Edmonton).

Big Bear

Because Big Bear and his band still lived on the northern edge of the plains near Jackfish Lake, McDougall said the Cree leader should go to the Fort Pitt meeting. Big Bear was not impressed. "We want none of the Queen's presents," he told McDougall. Distrustful and cautious, he saw the gifts as bait for a trap the government was preparing for the Cree.

As arranged, on August 18, 1876, government representatives and their interpreters came to Fort Carlton. Alexander Morris, the lieutenant-governor of the North West, spent a day explaining the terms of the treaty and assuring the assembled Cree that the Great Mother — Queen Victoria — thought of the plains peoples as her children. If they signed the treaty, she would give her Native children reserve lands, money, and gifts. She would send government men to help them settle and teach them how to raise potatoes and wheat. In return, she expected the Cree to respect the laws of the land. Though there was some dissent, the assembled chiefs signed the treaty, and Morris carried on to repeat the process at Fort Pitt.

Morris came to Fort Pitt armed not just with his treaty proposal, but with some strong opinions about the Cree leaders he was about to meet. George McDougall had told Morris that Big Bear was "an outsider, a troublesome fellow" who had no political power but great spiritual power, which he used to intimidate the other Cree chiefs. Because of McDougall's unfavourable opinion, Big Bear gained an undeserved reputation as a mischief-maker. Other Cree chiefs, notably Sweet Grass, had more favourable standing with McDougall, even though Big Bear was a more senior and powerful leader than Sweet Grass.

When Morris arrived, he learned that many chiefs and their bands — including Big Bear — were on the plains hunting buffalo. There were more than 100 Cree lodges camped at Fort Pitt, but the vast majority belonged to Woods Cree, who seldom ventured onto the plains to hunt. The concerns of the Woods and Plains Cree bands were very different, but Morris had no way of knowing that. He only knew that Chief Sweet Grass was likely to sign the treaty and could sway the opinions of the other chiefs who were present. Morris decided to proceed.

A council was swiftly called among all the chiefs. Some of the council — Métis interpreter Peter Erasmus, for one — had been at Fort Carlton and could tell the others about what had happened there. Having acted as interpreter at Fort Carlton, Peter was in favour of the treaty and urged the chiefs to sign. They were inclined to agree. Without waiting for Big Bear, one by one, the Woods Cree chiefs put their marks on the document.

Big Bear

When Big Bear finally arrived at Fort Pitt, he was too late. The negotiations were over, though there was still time for him to sign the treaty before Morris departed. Big Bear tried to explain to Morris that the chiefs who had signed the treaty did not speak for the entire Cree nation. Big Bear told the governor that he would not sign the treaty until he had conferred with the Plains Cree not represented at Fort Pitt. The Woods Cree chiefs pressured him to give up his objections and sign. To this, Big Bear replied, "Stop, stop my friends. I have never seen the governor before. I will make a request that he will save me from what I most dread, the rope about my neck. It was not given to us by the Great Spirit that the red man or white man should shed each other's blood."

As was the custom of aboriginal peoples, Big Bear was speaking symbolically. He was afraid to lose his freedom and didn't want to be caught and tamed like a wild horse. He feared the ways of his people would be changed forever. But Peter Erasmus, an excellent translator, had already left Fort Pitt, and the person responsible for translating Cree into English made a complete hash of Big Bear's words. The interpreter told Morris that Big Bear wanted assurance that no Native person would ever be hanged for the murder of a white person. Morris was outraged and proceeded to reprimand Big Bear, who must have wondered what on earth the governor was talking about.

Big Bear adamantly refused to sign until he had conferred with other Plains Cree chiefs and with members of his own band. He clearly understood that the buffalo were disappearing, that his people were suffering from disease, starvation, and the effects of whisky — all the disasters foretold by the disappearance of the Iron Stone and in his own long-ago vision. He knew something had to be done, but what? He was opposed to taking a reserve and settling down. Instead, he wanted to find a way to protect the buffalo, and to preserve Cree traditions and freedoms. He was determined to find a solution, but could not see what that solution might be. Meanwhile, he refused to sign the treaty. It would prove to be the costliest decision of his life.

For the next six years, Big Bear continued to hold out against Treaty Six. He continued to believe that signing the treaty would be the death of his people, that they would be forced onto a reserve, abandoned, and forgotten. He was also convinced that unless all Native peoples of the plains stood together in solidarity and demanded better treatment, their cause would fail. For his courageous stand, his reputation as a troublemaker continued to grow, and the government would not negotiate with him. He waited in vain to get a better deal for his people.

Big Bear

Meanwhile, his people descended into poverty and starvation. Although other Cree bands weren't much better off, at least those who signed the treaty and took reserve lands were entitled to food rations and treaty payments. Not so Big Bear and his followers. They were left without assistance. The pressure on Big Bear to affix his name to the treaty was intense. His people were destitute and he could save them, if only he would sign!

Like other bands of the Blackfoot and Cree, Big Bear led his band south of the Canada–United States border in search of buffalo. They stayed in Montana for a time, but in April 1882, he brought his people back to camp near Fort Walsh in the Cypress Hills, in southwestern Saskatchewan. Big Bear had still not signed Treaty Six so he and his band were not entitled to the daily rations that the NWMP were handing out to the others camped at Fort Walsh.

The Cree were starving, but Big Bear's family and followers were the most destitute of all. His band had nothing to eat. They huddled in ripped tipis that let in the wind and rain and wore the barest of shreds and rags. Big Bear hung on, despite the pleas of his family to sign the treaty so they could have whatever meagre rations the government was handing out.

He would not sign.

Things went from bad to worse. Finally, a woman of his band had enough. Her children were crying from hunger and she couldn't stand it any more. This woman — Big Bear's own daughter — went behind her chief's back and signed the treaty. Many of the band members followed her lead, including another of Big Bear's daughters and two of his sons, Twin Wolverine and Imasees.

Then on December 8, 1882, it seemed that the old chief's iron will had broken. Big Bear walked into the Indian agent's office at Fort Walsh, in the company of those brave and determined Cree who continued to stand with him. Wrapped in a torn blanket, he stood in silence. Then he began to speak. He explained — once again — his position: that the Cree, so accustomed to roving the plains in search of the buffalo, so used to the wind, sun, and snow, could not simply forget their old ways and become farmers overnight. They would need assistance and patience. They were weak and hungry. They were like lost children. But the government ignored them and treated them like criminals when all they wanted was food.

Big Bear's speech continued for four hours. At last, he could talk no more. His heart was empty. Big Bear signed the treaty.

Trouble Brewing

The following June, Big Bear and several other Cree leaders folded what little remained of their camp and left Fort Walsh. Accompanied by Indian agent Thomas Quinn, and a detachment of mounted police, some 500

Cree began a three-week walk to their new reserve lands on the North Saskatchewan River.

But Big Bear was angry. As he walked, he stomped his fury into the hard ground. He had signed the treaty just six months earlier, but already government had lied. According to the treaty terms, Big Bear was supposed to choose his reserve lands. But the government arbitrarily decided he should settle at Frog Lake, near Fort Pitt. When his band reached the Poundmaker reserve near Battleford, Big Bear halted and refused to proceed to Frog Lake. He and his band remained on the Poundmaker reserve until the spring of 1884. Because of his defiant action, the government refused to hand over the rations to which Big Bear and his band were entitled — another broken promise!

For those Cree leaders who had signed Treaty Six, conditions were almost as bad. The Canadian economy was in a tailspin and the government could not honour the treaty commitments. To save money, rations were reduced, and many of the Indian agents and farm instructors lost their jobs. Big Bear's fears were coming true: the plains people were being abandoned at the very moment when they most needed help.

All that winter, while he stayed on Poundmaker's reserve, Big Bear's discontent festered and grew into a rage that he could barely contain. He wanted so badly to unite the entire Cree nation, to speak out with one clear, loud voice that the government could not ignore.

Big Bear decided to hold a Thirst Dance to call together as many Cree as possible. They would sing and dance; they would pray and chant. They would speak together in councils. They would unite. They would cry out in a mighty yell together. This was his dream.

Big Bear sent messengers far and wide over the plains, with tobacco and an invitation to come to Poundmaker's reserve. Discontented and hungry, many Cree and even Blackfoot answered the call. By June 1884, about 2000 plains people had travelled to the reserve to join the Thirst Dance. Big Bear walked among them. He may have smiled to see his people laughing, to see children playing, to see women sharing what little food they had for their families. But what he really wanted was for the men to talk, not of war or rebellion, but to talk of how they would beat the Canadian government at its own game, the game of politics.

Big Bear did not want bloodshed or violence. Around the Thirst Dance's night fires, the dissatisfaction and anger, the distrust and hard feelings rose among the young Cree warriors. The burrs of lies, meagre rations, and lost buffalo got under the skins of the young men and they began to speak of war. During the Thirst Dance, some young men went to get their daily rations, but the Indian agent refused them. One of the young Cree hit the agent with an axe handle. The fearful agent immediately reported the incident to the mounted police detachment in nearby Battleford. Two officers were dispatched to find the offending young men and bring them in to the jailhouse.

The officers rode out to the reserve to make their arrest. The Thirst Dance was in progress. All around, the police saw a whirl of painted faces and angry eyes. The agent could not recognize the young man who hit him. A bristling, ferocious crowd pressed around the agent and the two officers. Tension was thick as smoke, when Big Bear calmly told the officers he would find the young men and bring them to Battleford after the dance was over. The police did not like this proposal but had no choice. They quickly left the dance and headed to the agent's ration house. They sent a messenger to Battleford asking for help; reinforcements arrived over night.

The next day, Big Bear and another Cree leader, Poundmaker, offered themselves for arrest in place of the hotheaded young warriors, but the police refused. A crowd had assembled a short distance away, and the officers were certain they could find the suspects. Foolishly, they rode into the crowd. One man came forward to explain the events that led to the assault, but instead of listening to him, the officers began hauling him back to their cabin. That lit the fuse.

The assembled Cree, with an angry scream borne of starvation, fear, and anger, charged forward. They knocked the officers from their horses and grabbed their weapons. The situation was set to explode, but in the midst of the mêlée, a strong voice rose. It was Big Bear urging his Cree warriors to calm down, to think. It was a message of peace.

The police made it to the safety of the ration house. Barricaded inside, the commanding officer suddenly thought of a way to end the hostilities: offer food. As the message spread that the police were handing out rations, the heat of the moment cooled.

Trouble Boils Over

Eventually, after enduring a bitter winter on the Poundmaker reserve, Big Bear and his band wearily drifted north to Frog Lake. They camped on another Cree reserve in March of 1885. By now, Big Bear wanted to be left alone to follow the old ways as best he could. Though the old chief seemed content to spend his days hunting, the young men of his band remained restless and angry. They did not want to lay down their ambitions for war. One man in particular spoke out hotly about rebellion and revenge. It was the band's war chief,

Wandering Spirit, and he had the ear of the young warriors of Big Bear's camp.

In late March, while Big Bear went into the bush to
trap, his son Imasees took over as chief. Relations
between Imasees and Big Bear had been strained ever
since Imasees signed Treaty Six behind his father's back.
Imasees, now chief of the band in all but name, was
among the young men who heeded the defiant words of
Wandering Spirit. Big Bear returned from his hunt and
learned that Louis Riel and the Métis nation were in
open revolt against the government. A local Indian
agent, Thomas Quinn, asked Big Bear to make sure the
restless young men of his band did not use the Métis
rebellion as an opportunity to take up arms themselves.
Big Bear replied, "My word as chief does not carry the
weight it once did, but I will do what I can."

The young men started a war dance, and
Wandering Spirit incited them to attack the nearby set-
tlemen of Frog Lake. He said, "Tomorrow I will eat two-
legged meat [kill a man]. If you don't want to join me, go
home and put on your wives' dresses." Following his
lead, the warriors stopped their dancing and singing.
They crept in the dark, through the woodlands to the
tiny settlement, where they arrived in the early hours of
Sunday, April 2, 1885. While some of the warriors forced
their way into the settlers' homes, others went to the

HBC store and grabbed whatever goods they wanted. Big Bear was among them, telling them to stop, but the warriors ignored him.

Meanwhile, the settlers were herded into the village's church where, incredibly, the two Roman Catholic priests were allowed to conduct a brief mass. Big Bear stood at the back, hoping his presence would calm the situation. Wandering Spirit was also there with a rifle in his hands. The atmosphere inside the tiny log building was electric with tension. The settlers, not knowing what would happen next, shook with fear as they prayed.

Finally the sermon ended. Wandering Spirit ordered the settlers back to the Cree camp as prisoners. The women and some of the men did as they were told and began walking out of the village, but Thomas Quinn refused to obey. Nose to nose, the two men argued. Suddenly, in a single, fluid movement, Wandering Spirit stepped back, raised his gun, and shot Quinn in the head. The Frog Lake massacre had begun.

On hearing shots in the village behind them, the other settlers screamed and began to run. The Cree warriors followed them into the bush and killed them. Big Bear ran after his young men, crying out for them to stop the killing, but the situation was out of his control. The war chief, Wandering Spirit, was in command now.

Big Bear could only shout helplessly, his voice lost in the crack of rifle fire and the screams of the victims.

Two of the men were shot at close range as their terrified wives looked on. John Gowanlock died in his wife's arms but the Cree fighters forced her to abandon his body. One of the priests knelt over the body of another man. Wandering Spirit shot and wounded the priest, then another Cree warrior killed the clergyman with a second shot. In all, nine men, including the two Roman Catholic fathers, were gunned down. The remaining settlers became prisoners of Wandering Spirit, except for a young man who escaped and dashed to Fort Pitt, where he informed the NWMP detachment that Big Bear's band of Cree had joined the Riel Rebellion.

Wandering Spirit now led his followers eastward to Fort Pitt to confront the police. He planned for the Cree to get food and ammunition, then carry on to the Battleford district, where more Cree would join them. With their prisoners in tow, it took many days to reach Fort Pitt. They arrived on April 14 by which time a HBC trader estimated there were 250 warriors. They surrounded the flimsy fort and demanded that the mounted police abandon it and leave the settlers as hostages.

The NWMP officer in charge at Fort Pitt was Frances Dickens, son of the famous author, Charles

Dickens. Though there was some shooting — two police constables were killed — Big Bear managed to negotiate a ceasefire long enough for the police to escape. Dickens and his men piled onto crude rafts and scurried down the North Saskatchewan River to Battleford, leaving some 40 defenceless villagers behind. The settlers were taken prisoner and the warriors looted their homes as well as the HBC storehouse. They then burned Fort Pitt to the ground and headed back to their camp at Frog Lake, prisoners in tow.

The Pursuit of Big Bear
Because he was known to the public as the troublesome leader of the Cree, Big Bear was blamed for the Frog Lake massacre, the sacking and two murders at Fort Pitt, plus the long chase and two fierce bush battles that followed. Yet with the war council of Wandering Spirit in control of the band, the weary old chief was no more than a follower, powerless and without influence. The man who wanted only peace and a better life for his people was hunted mercilessly through the dense, boggy woodlands. Some 25 kilometres north of Fort Pitt, the Cree and their hostages made camp near a prominent hill known as Frenchman's Butte. The warriors danced and sang victory songs, although they knew that soldiers were following them.

All the way from Calgary, under the command of General Thomas Strange, a combined force of mounted police, professional soldiers, and barely-trained militia headed north to put down the Cree rebellion. The Canadian army, led by General Middleton, was busy dealing with Riel so it fell to Strange and his troops to bring the Cree to surrender and free their prisoners. The man Strange most wanted to capture was Big Bear.

The troops caught up with the Cree at Frenchman's Butte. Wandering Spirit had his warriors dig trenches in the hillside. From this vantage point, the Cree fighters could fire down on the advancing soldiers. Although the Cree had a tremendous tactical advantage, their weapons were old. The soldiers had cannons, which they trained on the hillside and fired. Outgunned, the Cree warriors abandoned their rifle pits and fled over the hilltop. Instead of pressing after them, Strange was short of ammunition and also withdrew.

In the Cree camp, it was pandemonium. The fighters came flying over the hill, crying that the soldiers were coming. Women and children, the elderly and sick, the hostages, and others — including Big Bear — were tensely waiting. They fled into the bush. Wandering Spirit led them northward. He advised the band to use many different trails to confuse the pursuing soldiers, and he set fires and pushed over trees to create barriers and distractions. The band travelled swiftly and finally reached the shores of Loon Lake, 60 kilometres away.

Strange followed doggedly, but the going was slow. He sent the militia on ahead, under the command of NWMP Inspector Sam Steele. Clad in his red police tunic and leading a motley crew of cowboys who became known as Steele's Scouts, Steele caught up with the Cree at a spot where Loon Lake narrows to a marshy strait of water, backed by dense pine forest. Again, the Cree fought, but exhaustion and panic overcame them and they began to run across the narrow neck of water and into the woods. The soldiers did not pursue them.

In the confusion that followed, the Cree split up. Wandering Spirit abandoned the main band and turned west. Big Bear's son, Imasees, gained control of the remaining Cree and their hostages. He led them, at first, to the northeast. But when Imasees and his warriors decided to make a run for the U.S. border, Big Bear dug in his heels, refusing to follow his son. Gradually, small groups of Cree defected from Big Bear's group but the old chief, fearing for his life, kept going. In the end, his only companions were his son, Horse Child, and a faithful friend named Two and Two. Together, the three fugitives wandered in the northern woods, frightened, tired, and destitute. This brave old man, who once spoke for an entire nation, was now virtually alone in the wilderness — and, with Louis Riel already behind bars, public attention focused with intensity on Big Bear.

On July 4, 1885, his face deeply lined with worry and struggle, Big Bear walked out of the bush and surrendered at Fort Carlton.

"The Rope Around My Neck"

If the pursuit of Big Bear had been relentless, his trial was equally so. The public wanted justice and Big Bear's name was well known. Even though Big Bear was not the war chief and was not in control of the decisions made at Frog Lake, Fort Pitt, Frenchman's Butte, or Loon Lake, he was public enemy number one. He had once spoken about his fear of "the rope around my neck," referring to the loss of his freedom. Now, standing trial for his part in the Cree uprising, it seemed inevitable that he would soon feel a real rope around his neck.

Upon his surrender, Big Bear was transported to Regina to stand trial, which was set for September 11, 1885. Big Bear was charged with felony treason. He was not, however, charged with any of the murders at Frog Lake or Fort Pitt. A man named Beverley Robertson defended him and D. L. Scott was the Crown's prosecutor. Hugh Richardson was the judge. Six men sat in the jury box, hearing evidence.

Robertson did his best to discredit the Crown's case

against Big Bear. He tried to show that Big Bear was not in control of the band, that Imasees and Wandering Spirit were the real culprits. Despite testimony that supported Robertson's case, the public image of Big Bear as a cruel and calculating leader was too strong in the jury's minds. They convicted Big Bear, and he was sentenced to three years in prison in Winnipeg.

On hearing the verdict, Big Bear spoke — but his voice was raised not on his own behalf. Instead he pleaded for the welfare of his people. "I always thought it paid to do all the good I could. Now my heart is on the ground. I am dead to my people. Many of my band are hiding in the woods, paralysed with terror. Cannot this court send them a pardon? My own children, perhaps they are starving and outcast, afraid to appear in the light of day. If the government does not come to them with help before the winter sets in, my band will surely perish."

Big Bear was a quiet prisoner. He spent as much time as he could tending the prison's farm animals. After a year, many of the other Cree, who had been convicted of various crimes during the 1885 rebellion, had been released, but the government — and the public — were disinclined to let Big Bear go before his sentence was served. He stayed behind while Poundmaker and others went home. By the end of 1886, Big Bear, now in his 60s, fell ill. Finally, the prison doctors pressured the government to let him go. On January 27, 1887, Prime Minister Sir John A. Macdonald officially pardoned Big Bear.

But going back to his band was almost as bad as being in prison. His family was gone. His son Imasees had fled to Montana. His wife had left him. His people shunned him. Once a proud and caring man, Big Bear spent most of his remaining days in gloomy silence. He lived the last year of his life in lonely retreat, in the lodge of his daughter, Earth Woman, on the Poundmaker reserve.

Weary, broken hearted, painfully aware that the terrible vision of his youth had come true, Big Bear died in his sleep on January 17, 1888.

Chapter 3
Poundmaker
(Pitikwahanapiwiyin)

In the tradition of the plains First Nations, it was not unusual for a young person to be adopted by the chief of another band. The custom was often used to create alliances between bands. But when Crowfoot, the famous Blackfoot chief, adopted a young Cree man named Poundmaker, he astonished two entire nations.

Poundmaker knew tragedy early in his life, but the experience taught him about generosity and caring for the needy. He was a quiet and thoughtful person and a good hunter, even as a boy. He was also musical, adept at drumming and storytelling. He was gentle with children, courteous, and respectful with elders. He had a commanding physical presence; slender with waist-length hair; he stood more than six feet six inches tall. As a young man, Poundmaker was known as a fierce warrior. Later in life, he became an astute politician and exceptional speaker.

The Orphan

Poundmaker was born around 1840, in the Fort Carlton area north of present-day Saskatoon. His mother was Cree, but may have had French blood too. His father was a Stoney who lived among the Plains Cree. He was greatly esteemed as a buffalo caller — someone with skill in attracting and luring buffalo into the rough corrals or "pounds" constructed to confuse and trap them. The buffalo caller was known as Pitikwahanapiwiyin (pound maker), a name he also gave to his son.

Poundmaker had an older brother, Yellow Mud Blanket, and a younger sister. Their father died when the children were young so their mother returned to her parents. Within a few years, their mother and both grandparents also died, leaving the children homeless. A generous family took in the three orphans. Yellow Mud Blanket and Poundmaker worked hard to hunt and help provide enough meat for their adopted family.

Like other young men of his band, Poundmaker spent his youth as a free-roaming warrior, stealing horses and raiding enemies. He married young and gave up his fighting ways to raise a family. Soon he also married his wife's sister, a common practice. Poundmaker settled into a happy life of hunting, and he became a councillor to Red Pheasant, chief of his band. Then a remarkable event changed Poundmaker's life.

Although the Cree and Blackfoot were bitter enemies, there was talk of peace between the nations. In fact, the famous Blackfoot leader, Crowfoot, had personally come to Red Pheasant's band to bring gifts of tobacco and to talk of peace. While they were camped among the Cree, Crowfoot's wife noticed a tall young man who alarmed her greatly. He looked almost exactly like the son she and Crowfoot had recently lost — he was killed by a Cree war party. She called Crowfoot to meet the young man. Crowfoot, too, was stunned by Poundmaker's appearance.

To the amazement of everyone in Red Pheasant's band, Crowfoot invited Poundmaker to return with him to his Blackfoot camp. Poundmaker accepted and rode with the Blackfoot leader across the plains to the Oldman River. When Poundmaker became an honoured guest in Crowfoot's lodge, the young men of Crowfoot's band were angry and resentful. They plotted revenge against Poundmaker, thinking they could lure him away from his protector and swiftly murder him. But they feared Crowfoot's wrath, even more so when their chief announced that he had adopted Poundmaker as his son. Crowfoot gave Poundmaker a Blackfoot name, Wolf Thin Legs, and thus began a close and loving relationship that lasted until Poundmaker's death many years later.

Poundmaker spent the winter of 1873–74 in the camp of his adoptive father. He then returned to his own people who lived to the northeast. He brought many presents, including several horses, to prove that Crowfoot had indeed adopted him. He also carried a message of peace. Crowfoot still wanted to put an end to the bloody raids and horse stealing between the two nations. He realized the Blackfoot, Cree, and other First Nations would have to unite to make their voices heard.

Poundmaker himself agreed with this assessment, but he knew it would be difficult to convince the Cree to give up their old fighting ways. Poundmaker's status and reputation among the Cree was greatly enhanced by his close relationship with Crowfoot. Here was a man who had spent the entire winter in the lodge of his people's arch enemy and not only survived, he came back with gifts, and bore a strange message: peace between the nations. Poundmaker visited many Cree camps on his way back to his own band. He countered distrust and suspicion with steady nerves, cool-headed judgment, and persuasive arguments.

Poundmaker

His association with Crowfoot, combined with his eloquence and leadership, brought even more status for Poundmaker. Though still a young man, he became a Cree chief shortly after his return from Crowfoot's camp.

A New Life

On August 18, 1876, Lieutenant-Governor Alexander Morris sat before a council of Cree chiefs who had gathered at Fort Carlton to sign a treaty with the Dominion government. Morris had spent the previous day explaining the treaty in terms simple enough to be easily translated. Now it was their turn to respond to his offers. Morris considered the treaty to be generous — the government would give a section of land (one square mile) for every family, and in addition would build schools, and supply farm implements, seed, and livestock. Yet when the strikingly tall man named Poundmaker rose to speak, the Cree man was angry. "The governor mentions how much land is given to us. He says 640 acres for each family, he will give us. This is our land! It isn't a piece of pemmican to be cut off and given in little pieces back to us. It is ours and we will take what we want."

Poundmaker went on. "I beg of you to assist me in every way possible. When I am at a loss how to proceed I want the advice and assistance of the government. The children yet unborn, I wish you to treat them in like manner as they advance in civilization like the white man."

It was a classic case of underestimation on one side, misunderstanding on the other. Morris had no authority to alter the treaty or offer more than he had already stated. The Cree were there to negotiate, not to simply accept the treaty without question. They did not realize that Morris had already put all his cards on the table; he had nothing more to offer them. He certainly could not promise what Poundmaker was requesting. Morris hedged and offered to give the Cree such assistance as may be required in the event of a disaster. Though Poundmaker remained reluctant, with this reassurance in place, he and the other Cree chiefs signed the treaty and Morris went on to Fort Pitt.

The next three years were difficult for Poundmaker and all the Cree people. Despite signing Treaty Six, Poundmaker did not take a reserve right away. He and his band continued to follow the buffalo. But the buffalo were disappearing more quickly than anyone would have believed. Finally, with the herds diminished and his people starving, Poundmaker ushered his band south into Montana to find food. They remained south of the border until 1879, when a skirmish with the American cavalry convinced Poundmaker to return to Canada. He journeyed north and took a reserve on the Battle River, close to the tiny settlement of Battleford.

Here, he and his people resigned themselves to learning a new life. Seeing that their only salvation would be to give up their old ways, Poundmaker tried to set an example for his band by working hard to grow

crops and erect fences for cattle. The band still depend-
ed on government rations, but they were making an
effort to become self-sufficient farmers. In the spring of
1880, as promised in the treaty, livestock, seed, and farm
implements were brought to Poundmaker's reserve.

With members of his band looking on, he hitched a
team of oxen and prepared to plough some land for
seeding. The farm instructor advised Poundmaker to
find one or two stout men to add their weight to the
plough's cross beam because the virgin prairie would
resist the blade. Poundmaker's friend Mustatamus vol-
unteered. Poundmaker commanded the oxen to move
forward. Nothing happened. Exasperated, the chief
called for someone to get the team moving. Eager to
comply, two men jumped up and began whooping and
yelling. The startled oxen jumped forward. The plough
blade struck an unseen rock, throwing Poundmaker and
Mustatamus backward, while the ox team, now totally
terrified, took off across the field. To much laughter, the
team was captured and several more Cree men came
forward to help. Time and again the plough jammed
against rocks and roots, but Poundmaker was determined. The onlookers laughed and cheered — and the
field, at last, was ploughed and ready for planting.

The men of Poundmaker's band went hunting
while the crops grew. They caught anything they could

— rabbits, deer, prairie chickens — and kept alert for signs of buffalo. But the huge herds were gone, never to return. The people preserved what meat they could, harvested grain and root crops in the fall, and scraped though the winter.

The Letter and the Battle
In the early spring of 1885, the situation on Poundmaker's reserve became one of unrest. The band was divided. Poundmaker continued working hard to learn farming. But no matter how hard he tried to adopt a new way of life, he could not keep hunger from stalking his people. They were still receiving daily rations, yet the people were continually on the brink of starvation. Like the young men of Big Bear's camp, the young men on Poundmaker's reserve did not like farming. They did not want to give up the old ways. They were restless and angry and ready for a fight.

In March, news of the Métis rebellion came to Battleford, and the settlers there became nervous. With seven Cree reserves in the area, would Battleford be the next location of an uprising? The settlers learned of the massacre at Frog Lake and the burning of Fort Pitt. Tension filled the air like dust. So when Poundmaker sent a message that he and two other chiefs were on their way to Battleford to speak with Indian agent John

Rae, the townspeople and the surrounding farmers feared the worst. Some 500 people barricaded themselves inside the mounted police post and warily awaited Poundmaker's arrival.

On the morning of March 30, Poundmaker came to Battleford. He wanted to speak with Rae, first to reassure him that his band had no intention of joining the rebellion, secondly to press Rae for more farm implements, seed, and rations. Poundmaker was there to plead for better conditions for his people, no doubt aware that the Riel Rebellion had handed the Cree a perfect opportunity to use the settlers' fear of a Native uprising as a bargaining position. The streets were deserted as the Cree leader and his supporters rode into town. Eventually they came to the police barracks and asked to speak with Rae, but the distrustful agent would not show himself, nor would he send the tea and tobacco that Poundmaker requested as a sign of good faith. Poundmaker waited patiently but by day's end Rae had done nothing.

And so it was that Poundmaker found himself in an empty, undefended town — and roving Cree warriors who were barely under his control. Finally, as darkness fell, the inevitable happened. The Cree fighters, who were hungry and dressed in rags, began looting the stores and houses, eating and drinking all night.

Poundmaker tried to stop the pillaging and destruction but the ball was rolling beyond his control. He left Battleford in disgust. By morning, the young men followed him, leaving the town ransacked and ruined.

In the police post, the settlers and townsfolk could hear the revelry and laughter outside. They telegraphed a desperate plea for help. In Swift Current, far to the south, General Fred Middleton was leading the Canadian army in a march northward to do battle with Riel and the Métis. Upon receiving news of the siege at Battleford, Middleton dispatched Lieutenant-Colonel W. D. Otter and his troops to proceed immediately to Battleford and restore order.

For many days after their initial spree, Cree warriors kept returning to the town to replenish their supplies of food, drink, and ammunition. They burned several stores and houses. Yet, according to Robert Jefferson, the area's farm instructor (who was married to Poundmaker's sister), the Cree only wanted to speak to agent Rae and negotiate with him. Jefferson, who remained in the Cree camp throughout the troubles in Battleford, later wrote that the Cree warriors never mounted an organized attack on Battleford. They simply took advantage of the situation to get food, blankets, and whisky.

Meanwhile, Métis leader, Louis Riel, was in trouble.

His Métis fighters were vastly outnumbered by Middleton and the Canadian troops. He needed reinforcements. He needed the Cree.

Two days after the siege of Battleford started, Métis messengers visited Poundmaker's camp, telling tales of courage and great deeds, leading the young Cree warriors to believe that Riel had the upper hand. The Cree would realize their ambitions if only they would join Riel's forces. In fact, the opposite was true. Poundmaker wisely saw through the messengers' rhetoric.

Like Big Bear far to the northeast, Poundmaker was no longer in control of his band. The warrior society, full of headstrong young fighters, was running the camp now. A Métis messenger named Jobin, rode into the camp and taunted the warriors. Jobin suggested the Cree war society should send a letter to Riel, telling him that they would come. Robert Jefferson was summoned to write the letter. Poundmaker stepped inside the lodge, but sat quietly, taking no part in the discussion or the letter that Jobin dictated. Jobin told Jefferson to write that the Cree were anxious to join Riel and would be no more than four days on the trail. Jobin added a number of wild stories, including a claim that the Cree intended to take Battleford. Then Jobin told Jefferson to write Poundmaker's name at the bottom of the letter.

On April 24, Lieutenant-Colonel Otter and almost

500 troops arrived in Battleford to the thankful cheers of the relieved residents who had been holed up in their crowded fort for more than three weeks. Otter had no authority to pursue the Cree — he was simply to keep the peace in Battleford — but he took matters into his own hands and set out to find and punish Poundmaker. Otter and 325 soldiers began their march.

The next day, May 2, 1885, Otter drew near the Cree camp. He thought he would surprise the Cree with an attack at dawn, but the Cree knew exactly what was going on and moved to the west side of Cut Knife Hill, a long, gentle slope that was scored by a series of deep ravines. As the soldiers crossed the creek and approached the slope, Cree warriors were waiting in the ravines, hidden by bush. The troops noticed some of these snipers and opened fire. The army was completely exposed on the slope's open ground. Receiving fire on all sides from an enemy they could not see, the soldiers believed they were greatly outnumbered, but actually, there were only 50 Cree fighters.

The Cree gradually moved around behind the soldiers. The troops were almost surrounded when Otter realized what was happening. He ordered a hasty retreat. The soldiers ran down the hill in disarray and panic. Mounted Cree warriors were ready to follow, but Poundmaker stepped forward saying, "They have come here to fight us and we have fought them. Now let them go."

Two days later, Jobin returned with more news from Riel and another request to send fighters. Poundmaker was furious. In the midst of a council meeting, he called Jobin a liar and blamed the Métis for the trouble at Battleford and the resulting battle at Cut Knife Hill. He told the assembly that he intended to take his family to seek sanctuary in the hills. But the Cree warriors, fuelled by their rout of Otter and his troops, chose to join Riel. With threats, armed Métis fighters forced Poundmaker and his followers to travel eastward to where Riel was waiting. Throughout this journey, though a virtual prisoner himself, Poundmaker took great care to ensure the safety of Jefferson, the missionary Father Cochin, and several other hostages.

When they were in the Eagle Hills, about 100 kilometres south of Battleford, the Cree learned the Canadian army had crushed the rebellion and Riel was under arrest. What would the Cree warriors do now? Would they continue their own fight? Would they run for the U.S. border? Would they surrender? A council was called. One by one, each man stood to give his opinion. At last, it was Poundmaker's turn.

Poundmaker tried to make the angry ones see reason. He said, "Today, it is no more a question of fighting.

You who have committed murders, who have plundered the innocents, it is no more time to think of saving your own lives. Look at all these women and children. Look at all these youths around you. They are all clamouring for their lives. It is a case of saving them. I know we are all brave. If we keep on fighting the whites, we can embarrass them. But we will be overcome by their numbers, and nothing tells us that our children will survive. I would sooner give myself up and run the risk of being hanged than see my tribe and children shot through my fault, and by an unreasonable resistance see streams of blood. Now, let everyone who has a heart do as I do and follow me."

The council agreed.

Poundmaker asked his brother-in-law, Robert Jefferson, to write a letter to General Middleton, asking for various terms and conditions of the Cree's surrender. Jefferson rode away and delivered the letter, but Middleton exploded into a sputtering rage and denied that any terms would be extended to Poundmaker. It would be unconditional surrender or war. Jefferson returned to Poundmaker with this news. With a heavy heart, the Cree leader took his people north to Battleford to lay down their arms.

A dignified leader, a man of peace, Poundmaker faced Middleton. He first gave the general his rifle, then extended his hand in a sign of friendship. Middleton haughtily spurned the outstretched hand. Instead, he had Poundmaker arrested and put into chains.

The Trial

On July 4, 1885, Poundmaker and several other Native leaders were sent to Regina for trial. Charged with felony treason, he pleaded not guilty. He was defended by Beverley Robertson. Six witnesses spoke in his defence versus nine for the prosecution. One of the prosecutor's witnesses was none other than Robert Jefferson, Poundmaker's brother-in-law.

The Crown prosecutor, Scott, opened his arguments by presenting the damning letter to Riel, written on April 29 at Cut Knife Hill and apparently signed by Poundmaker. Then Jefferson took the witness stand. Under questioning, he related to the jury how he had written the letter to Riel exactly as Jobin had told him to. But Jefferson's testimony became uncertain when he was asked whether Poundmaker himself took any part in dictating the letter. To further cloud his own evidence, Jefferson revealed that another Cree warrior told him to affix Poundmaker's name to the letter — and after all the chiefs had signed, the Métis appeared to have made changes to the text. The letter, which at first seemed to be strong evidence against Poundmaker, was shown to be the flimsy collection of lies that it was. Scott moved on, calling NWMP Superintendent Herchmer to the stand.

Herchmer testified that he had seen Poundmaker twice during the battle, once from at least 1500 metres, the second time from some three kilometres away. Herchmer told the jury he could not be certain what Poundmaker was doing, but ventured the opinion that the Cree leader was giving directions to the warriors. Scott also brought forth evidence about Poundmaker's supposed part in the siege of Battleford.

For his defence, Robertson tried to make the jury understand the inner workings of Cree society, and that the chief or leader usually gives up his authority to a war chief in times of battle. He tried to show that Poundmaker was not in control of the band. Neither did he make decisions about whether or not to join Riel, to loot and burn Battleford, or to fight Otter and the Canadian army at Cut Knife Hill. Robertson also tried to establish Poundmaker as a man of peace and reason, using several witnesses who knew the chief well and could vouch for his character.

It was all in vain. After only a few minutes of deliberation, the jury pronounced Poundmaker guilty. The judge then allowed Poundmaker to speak. He said, "I am not guilty. Much has been said against me that is not true. Everything I could do was done to prevent blood-shed. Had I wanted war, I would not be here now, I would be on the prairie. You did not catch me; I gave myself up. You have got me, because I wanted peace."

Prison and Freedom

Poundmaker was sentenced to three years in the Stony Mountain Penitentiary in Winnipeg. His health deteriorated from the beginning of his imprisonment. After only nine months, his state of health was so alarming that the Canadian government pardoned him and he was released. He went back to his reserve near Battleford to find his people broken in body and spirit. Poundmaker had no authority. Though his people welcomed him home, the government would not allow him to resume his position as chief. Disheartened, Poundmaker decided to visit Crowfoot. He left his family and his band on May 7, 1886. They never saw him again.

Accompanied by Stony Woman, his third wife, Poundmaker walked across the plains. The weather was cool and rainy. By the time he reached Blackfoot Crossing and Crowfoot's reserve, Poundmaker was ill and weak. Crowfoot and his band were as destitute as any of the plains peoples, but the Blackfoot leader welcomed his old friend and adopted son. Poundmaker recovered his strength over the next few weeks, and the two men spent much time talking and smoking.

It was early summer. The Blackfoot people were gathered for their annual Sun Dance. There are many stories about what happened on July 4, in the midst of the celebrations. One story alleges that Poundmaker collapsed while dancing. Another claims he and Crowfoot were taking a ceremonial meal together, when Poundmaker began to cough violently. Still another declares Poundmaker was making a speech to a group of Blackfoot, when he suddenly fell to the ground, unconscious. All the stories agree Poundmaker died within a few minutes of the first sign of trouble. The accepted theory is that a blood vessel burst in his weakened lungs and he died of severe blood loss before the horrified eyes of his loving stepfather Crowfoot. Poundmaker was just 44.

He was buried at Blackfoot Crossing on a slope overlooking the Bow River. Crowfoot died only a few years later. He, too, was buried at this spot. But the Cree people wanted the bones of their chief and leader returned to them. In 1967, they moved Poundmaker and buried him again — on the long, gentle slope of Cut Knife Hill.

Chapter 4
Peter Erasmus

During his life, the remarkable Peter Erasmus was employed by Methodist missionaries as a teacher, translator, hunter, and guide. He was an interpreter and guide for the famous Palliser Expedition. He made a tidy sum of money in gold mining, then lost it all to unfortunate investments.

Peter lived for awhile among the Cree at Whitefish Lake. As well as Plains Cree, he spoke several other languages and could read Latin and Greek. He was the official translator at the signing of Treaty Six, which led to many years of employment as a government translator and Indian agent.

Peter Erasmus

Peter Erasmus was a tall, strong man. He was well educated and confident, shrewd and intelligent. Though he was not a chief or leader, he earned the trust of Native peoples, settlers and traders, missionaries, and politicians. Through his honesty, hard work, and resourcefulness, he was able to play more than one pivotal role in the turbulent times of the North West Territories.

Adventure in the North-West

Peter Erasmus was born June 27, 1833 on his father's farm near Fort Garry (Winnipeg). He was named Peter, after his Danish father. He was the fourth child born to Erasmus and his Métis wife Catherine, also known as Kitty. When Peter was young, his mother told him many stories and legends from her Ojibwa family. Through her, he developed a lifelong respect for Native peoples and an understanding of their cultures.

Young Peter grew strong and lean and was accustomed to hard outdoor work. At the age of seven, he started school, a six-kilometre trek from home. He was an excellent pupil, but his formal education lasted only a few years. Peter's father died unexpectedly when Peter was 13 or 14. He quit school to help on the farm, mostly looking after the livestock. But his life as a shepherd didn't last long.

Peter's uncle from Cumberland House (now known as The Pas) came to Peter's mother with a proposal. He was establishing a new Anglican mission and needed an assistant. He wanted to hire Peter, who would not only be paid to help at the mission's school, but would also receive additional education. It was a great opportunity. In May 1851, Peter arrived at his uncle's new mission. He worked as a teacher, instructing up to 30 Native children in the basics of reading, writing, and Bible study. He quickly learned their language — Cree — developing a skill that would be the cornerstone of his life and later adventures.

Peter was a good teacher and continued to excel in his own studies. His uncle, along with several other Church elders right up to the bishop, wanted him to enter ministerial college, but the idea of a lifelong devotion to church work didn't appeal to adventurous young Peter. His uncle, however, was so persuasive that Peter gave in and entered Anglican seminary school at Fort Garry in 1855. Peter tried hard to make the best of the situation, but by the end of his second term, he knew he was not destined to be a minister. Once again, fate stepped in to re-direct Peter's life.

He received an invitation from the Hudson's Bay Company factor at Fort Garry (the head trader at each post was called the "factor" in HBC terminology). When he arrived, the factor greeted Peter warmly, saying he had known Peter's father. Then he got down to business. Reverend Woolsey, the Methodist missionary at Fort Edmonton, needed a healthy, dependable young man to serve as a guide and interpreter. On the strength of his father's good standing as a former HBC employee and Peter's own attributes, the Fort Garry factor considered him a likely candidate for the job.

Stunned, Peter could only nod at this exciting prospect. Though he was trying hard to be a good student at the seminary college, he was unhappy. But this was a chance for adventure! He eagerly accepted the factor's offer, almost ignoring the man's warning that the bishop, who had sponsored Peter as a seminary student, would not be pleased with this turn of events. Despite the protests of the bishop and his uncle in The Pas, at 22, Peter quit the college and set out for Fort Edmonton.

Woolsey's Man
Peter took a boat up the North Saskatchewan River, bound for Edmonton. En route, he learned that Woolsey would actually meet him at Fort Pitt, some 130 kilometres east of Fort Edmonton. Peter stepped off the boat and into his new life in September 1856.

His adventures began right away. Woolsey had a number of horses with him, which he intended to use as pack and saddle animals. Although he was raised on a farm, Peter had little experience with horses, especially half-wild ones. Preparing to set out across the prairie the next morning, Woolsey saddled a horse for Peter, but when Peter approached, the horse pulled away, snorting and skittish. Peter was able to mount but the stubborn horse refused to move forward with this inexperienced greenhorn on his back. At last, a young Cree man gave Peter a few quick tips on managing the horse and off he went at a smart trot — much to the amusement of the gathered Cree audience.

On his second day, Peter got an education of a different kind. He and Woolsey came upon the scalped, mutilated bodies of several Cree who had been killed by Blackfoot warriors. For young Peter, it was a shocking introduction to the ongoing raids and warfare between the two nations.

Along with his new assistant, Woolsey spent the winter of 1856–57 at Fort Edmonton. He proved to be a kindly man and treated Peter not so much as an employee, but as a friend. Peter's duties left plenty of time for fishing and hunting expeditions with the other men living at the post. Peter's experience with dog teams made him a valuable asset to the HBC factor. He was also an experienced fiddle player, another handy skill.

In the spring of 1857, Woolsey and Peter set out for

Pigeon Lake, located southwest of Fort Edmonton — where Woolsey had a mission and a congregation of some 200 Cree. Here again, despite long hours labouring on the mission building and garden and translating Woolsey's sermons, Peter had lots of time to hunt and hone his skills as a tracker and scout. With summer's arrival, the Cree band broke up their winter camp and headed east to the prairie to hunt buffalo. Woolsey and Peter joined them. At every opportunity, Woolsey rode out to preach to other Cree bands camped on the plains. Peter was constantly at Woolsey's side, translating back and forth between Cree and English.

By summer's end, the Pigeon Lake Cree returned to their home camp at the lake and settled in for the winter. Peter passed much of his time joining the men on hunts, learning every detail he could absorb. But big game was scarce and the Cree were forced to venture onto the plains, once again in search of buffalo. Woolsey decided to accompany them, even though the cold took its toll on him. Woolsey was not a young man. He became very sick, possibly with pneumonia. Woolsey and Peter left their Cree friends and returned to Fort Edmonton, where they spent the remainder of the winter.

In January 1858, the factor at Fort Edmonton summoned Peter to his office. Once again, Peter's skills had come to the attention of an important person. Once again, his life was about to take an unexpected turn.

The Palliser Expedition

In 1857, the British government sent an expedition of scientists and explorers to evaluate and report on the West's resources and its suitability for settlement and agriculture. The man leading that fact-finding commission was Captain John Palliser. Working under him were Dr. James Hector, Thomas Blakiston, Eugene Borgeau, and several others — each hand picked for his particular background and skills.

Palliser requested the Fort Edmonton factor find a guide and interpreter. The factor offered the position to Peter. Coincidentally, Woolsey had just received a letter from his superiors, telling him to cut costs. Though he hated to lose Peter's services, it seemed the time was perfect for his assistant to take this new opportunity with Palliser.

Dr. James Hector arrived at Fort Edmonton in March 1858. Peter immediately liked this energetic, well-educated man. Hector was not only a medical doctor, but he had studied chemistry, botany, natural history, geology, and palaeontology. Hector gave Peter instructions and a long shopping list of supplies for the summer's explorations, then departed for Fort Carlton. As soon as the river ice broke in the spring, Peter was to take provisions, horses, and supplies to Fort Carlton.

By mid-April Peter was on his way. He set up a camp close to Fort Carlton and spent a few days hunting buffalo to furnish more meat for the expedition. When Palliser arrived, he assigned Peter a variety of general tasks, including care and feeding of the horses, setting up camp, hunting, guiding, and interpreting as needed. Specifically, Palliser assigned Peter to accompany Hector in his numerous forays. Peter's knowledge of the local landscape, birds, animals, and Native peoples was invaluable to Hector, who in turn taught Peter to use surveying equipment.

At last, the party set out, bound southward over the open prairie, passing through herds of buffalo along the way. Their progress was slow because the expedition members were noting every detail about the land and mapping it as they went. After a long time, they reached Old Bow Fort, west of present-day Calgary, where they rested for a few days. Palliser then divided the group into several smaller parties, each of which took a different route into the mountains. The parties were to meet again at Fort Edmonton.

In mid-August, they began their trek. In the group with Hector were Peter Erasmus, Eugene Borgeau (a botanist), two other assistants named Brown and Sutherland, and a Stoney man the group nicknamed

Nimrod because of his hunting prowess. The group travelled light with only three packhorses. Nimrod assured Hector they would find plenty of game in the mountains for fresh meat.

Hector followed the Bow River westward, passing the locations of present-day Canmore and Banff. One day, near Castle Mountain (west of Banff), Peter tracked and shot a deer, but only wounded it. He continued to follow it through the forest. He was so focused on finding the deer that he lost track of time. Suddenly it was dark — and Peter had no idea where he was. Realizing it would be pointless to try finding his way back to camp, Peter built a fire and spent a long, uncomfortable night alone in the woods.

Well into the mountains now, the group left the Bow River, crossing the continental divide via Vermilion Pass. The terrain was rough and their progress was slow. Frequently, Peter and the other men were required to dismount and chop a trail through dense brush and deadfall. Hector often halted the group's progress so he could take measurements, collect samples of rock, plants, and fossils, or climb mountains. The men also hunted constantly. Contrary to Nimrod's assurances, the group encountered very little game and food supplies were critically low.

Late in August, the group reached a point near the

present-day city of Golden, B.C., and turned eastward. They found a turbulent, silt-laden river and followed it upstream toward the divide. The route proved to be very difficult — a narrow canyon with steep slopes leading down to the thundering river roaring below them. At one point, one of the packhorses slipped into the river, taking the group's meagre food supplies with it into the frigid water. Hector, trying to rescue the animal, was kicked in the chest and fell to the ground. Alarmed, Peter and the other party members dashed over, but Hector did not respond to their calls.

There are a number of versions describing what happened next. According to one popular story, the group reluctantly concluded that Hector was dead. They dug a grave and were preparing to place Hector's body into the hole when the "corpse" suddenly woke up. According to Peter's own memoirs, the men carried Hector to a sheltered spot, where they made camp. Hector remained unconscious for most of the day. He eventually came around, and though his injury was extremely painful, his sense of humour was intact — he wryly named the stream Kicking Horse River.

The next morning, Hector was much better, but still in no shape to travel. Nimrod had gone out hunting. He limped back empty-handed, his ankle injured. With two members of the party unable to walk or ride, it was up to Peter to find food. He set off once again, this time looking for a herd of bighorn sheep that Nimrod had spotted. After some searching Peter located the sheep and crept up on them. He was able to get a shot away and killed a big ram. He carried the meat back to the hungry camp. But due to the fall rutting season, the ram's meat was rank with a musky odour and taste. It was inedible.

The party continued slowly up the river valley, climbing toward the divide. They found a patch of blueberries and feasted, though they still had no meat. The situation was desperate. Peter went out again the next day, but came back with only a partridge, from which Nimrod made soup using butt ends of candles for fat. At last, despite his swollen ankle, Nimrod hobbled into the woods to look for moose. Eventually the party heard a shot, and Peter scrambled off in the direction of the blast. The Stoney hunter had been lucky at last. Peter helped him carry much-needed meat back to the camp.

The rest of the trip was difficult, though relatively uneventful. Satisfied with his accomplishments, Hector proceeded eastward out of the mountains, following the North Saskatchewan River. They reached Fort Edmonton on October 7, having covered some 900 kilometres in 57 days.

Peter passed another winter at Fort Edmonton. In

the spring, Palliser was ready to set out again. He planned to explore the area that is now southern Saskatchewan and Alberta, after which, he intended to split the group. Like the previous summer, each small party would explore a different route through the mountains. They were to rendezvous at Fort Colville, an HBC outpost in what is now Washington. Here the men would be paid and Palliser and his British companions would journey west to Victoria to catch a boat for England.

For the second time, the group journeyed south, well into Blackfoot territory. They set up a base camp near the Canada–U.S. border. Peter and several others patrolled a large circle around the camp, scouting for evidence of Blackfoot. As they crested a hill, Peter spotted movement in the thick brush ahead. He told his companions to get their firearms ready, then they rode at a full gallop straight toward the spot, hoping to flush out the hidden warriors. The Blackfoot raiding party was taken completely by surprise. After a few minutes, when they were well away from the ambush, Peter noticed a pain in his leg. Looking down, he was astonished to see an arrow stuck in his calf. One of the other men cut off the long shaft, and Peter rode back to camp, where Hector patched him up.

The party had a number of other encounters with

Blackfoot, Blood, and Peigan bands. Though there were some testy moments, there was no further hostility. Palliser explored the terrain from the Rockies to Cypress Hills. The summer quickly waned, leaving little time for detailed mountain exploration. Though Hector asked Peter to accompany him into the Rockies, Peter declined, saying the food supply was too limited, the horses too tired, and the season too late.

Hector was furious, but Palliser supported Peter's decision, saying Peter had a perfect right to decline work he felt was too dangerous. Instead, Peter found his own way to Fort Colville to obtain his pay for two years' service on the Palliser Expedition. Hector ventured into the Rockies once again. Despite his disappointment that Peter was not with him, Hector named a peak in Peter's honour: 3265-metre Mt. Erasmus, near the Howse River.

Searching for Gold
Officially released from his employment with Palliser, Peter was at loose ends when he was approached by two men needing assistance on a gold prospecting venture. The men, Peter Whitford and Baptiste Anasse, offered Peter two-thirds of whatever gold they found. The catch: the prospectors had no money so Peter had to outfit the expedition out of his own pocket. He accepted their terms.

Peter Erasmus

Peter Erasmus

The trio set out for a spot where gold had been discovered. They were among the first to arrive at this remote location, somewhere north of Fort Colville (historians don't know exactly where). Within two weeks, there was a makeshift town of tents and shanties. The three set up camp, built themselves a small cabin, and spent the balance of the fall working their claims. As winter approached, the horses were finding less grass for grazing. Finally, Anasse left to take the horses back to Fort Colville for the winter, while Whitford and Peter remained behind to guard the claim.

Anasse arrived back at camp in the spring, but almost immediately, the two prospectors decided it was time to go back to Colville and cash in their gold. Whitford found some eager miners to buy the claims, and the trio made ready to leave. In full view of the claims' new owners, Whitford lifted a floorboard and withdrew two small pouches, presumably the gold that he and Anasse had amassed over the previous year's work. The partners mounted up and departed. They rode hard and made a simple camp with no campfire. Anasse set up a decoy camp a few hundred metres up the trail, complete with log dummies under warm blankets and a campfire. Next, the three partners hid in the woods and kept watch through the long, cold night.

Peter detected movement in the dark. At least two men were creeping toward the false camp. One of them raised a knife over a dummy and brought the weapon down hard. Anasse and Whitford began firing. The would-be murderers instantly disappeared into the night, running down the trail to a barrage of bullets.

Peter Erasmus

Whitford strode into the false camp and pulled a long blade out of the blanket-covered log that was supposed to be a sleeping Peter Erasmus. He handed the weapon to Peter as a souvenir. But the night's surprises weren't over yet. Whitford made his way to a nearby pile of rocks, which he flung aside to reveal a duffel bag — the gold that Anasse had hidden the previous November, when he took the horses to Colville.

Treaty Six

Peter returned to Fort Edmonton and spent the next few years working for his old employer, Reverend Woolsey. The Methodist church had established several missions among the Cree in a large region, northeast of Edmonton. At one of these missions, Peter met a young Cree woman, Charlotte, whom he married. Eventually Woolsey's health failed. He was replaced by Reverend George McDougall — the man responsible for taking the sacred Iron Stone. But when George McDougall threatened to reduce Peter's wages without taking a cut in pay himself, Peter quit.

Now married and without an income, Peter took to trapping and buffalo hunting to make money. The couple settled at Whitefish Lake, among a Cree band led by a chief named Pakan, also known as James Seenum. Peter ran a successful trapline and made several trips

81

down the North Saskatchewan, all the way to Fort Garry to see his family and trade his furs.

Then in 1876, two Cree chiefs, Big Child and Star Blanket, sent a message to Peter. The chiefs were to meet with representatives of the North West Mounted Police and the government of Canada to negotiate and sign a treaty. The Cree needed a trustworthy person to translate for them — to correctly interpret their wishes to the English-speaking government men. The chiefs asked Peter Erasmus to be their interpreter. Peter was honoured but reluctant to accept — Charlotte was about to have another child (their fifth) and Peter was uneasy about leaving her alone at such a time. But she insisted, telling him there were plenty of women in their Cree community who could look after her and the new baby.

Peter rode five long, hard days to reach Fort Carlton in time for the negotiations. As he was settling into his tipi, Big Child came to speak with him. The chief told Peter that the government had hired two other interpreters, but the Cree chiefs were determined to use Peter as their translator. The other two interpreters turned out to be Peter Ballenden and Reverend John McKay, both of whom had lived and worked among the Cree for many years. Peter knew both men, but he doubted the extent of their knowledge of the Plains Cree language. In particular, McKay spoke Woods Cree, distinctly different from the language of the plains peoples.

It was time for introductions and preliminaries to the treaty meeting. Along with the Cree chiefs and their councillors, Peter entered the tent where Lieutenant-Governor Alexander Morris and the other government men were seated. Big Child told Morris that the Cree had hired Peter as their interpreter, but Morris objected, saying that the government already had two competent translators on hand. Big Child replied, "You keep your two men, we will keep Peter to translate for us. We will pay him ourselves." (Peter was quick to translate Big Child's words into English for Morris.) Still Morris objected, until Big Child threatened to leave the negotiations. Again, Peter fluently translated the chief's speech. Just as the entire event was on the brink of dissolving, Morris relented.

In the morning, the chiefs and councillors assembled in Morris' large tent. Peter was summoned to the front table, where the government men were seated. He was bluntly told that he should translate Morris' opening speech. This Peter refused to do, saying he was employed by the Cree, not the government. After speaking in English, Peter translated his own words into Cree for the benefit of the chiefs. Big Child asked Peter whether he was capable of translating the governor's speech, to which Peter replied, "Certainly I can, or else I would not be here. Let their own men speak first, and you will understand why I refuse to do their bidding."

Morris began his speech with McKay interpreting. McKay's Woods Cree was peppered with words from other Native languages, especially Chippewa. Big Child was not impressed. Jumping to his feet, he shouted that the Plains Cree people wished to be addressed in their own language. McKay did his best to translate the chief's angry words but became confused and stopped speaking. Peter Ballenden, the other government translator, then stood. As Morris continued his opening remarks, Ballenden translated into Plains Cree, but he mumbled and could not be heard in the large tent. Finally, the frustrated Morris personally called upon Peter to translate.

And so Peter Erasmus became the official translator for the Treaty Six negotiations. After Morris explained the treaty terms (and Peter effectively translated) the Cree chiefs spent the balance of that day and night talking among themselves and forming their response. The next day they assembled again, and Morris invited them to give him their concerns and opinions.

Poundmaker was the first man to speak. While many of the chiefs were inclined to accept the treaty,

Poundmaker sought better terms. Morris gave a further explanation of the treaty terms, and the chiefs asked for another recess. The negotiations would resume in three days' time. Meanwhile, Peter was called into the chiefs' council meeting so that he would clearly understand the Cree's concerns before they went back to Morris. The talks continued throughout the day with Poundmaker leading the objectors, but in the end, the chiefs decided to accept the treaty.

The chiefs came, once again, to speak with Morris. The treaty terms were read. There was more discussion and another recess. Poundmaker and his supporters tried, once more, to get better terms in the treaty. Morris grudgingly agreed to some of these requests. At last, the discussion was complete. The Cree chiefs signed the treaty.

Morris called Peter into his tent and asked him to come to Fort Pitt for the second round of treaty discussions with the Cree of that area. Peter agreed. He arrived at Fort Pitt ahead of the government party and was quickly whisked into a council meeting of the chiefs to explain what had transpired at Fort Carlton. One of the chiefs, Sweet Grass, told the assembled leaders that he considered Big Child and Star Blanket to be wise. If the treaty was good enough for them, it would be good enough for him, too. He announced his intention to sign. Pakan, leader of Peter's own band from Whitefish Lake, also agreed. The next day, before Morris, all the chiefs in attendance repeated their support of the treaty, and the formalities were quickly completed. Peter was paid for his work. Still concerned about his wife, Peter soon left for home — a little too soon, as it turned out.

Big Bear, who had been hunting buffalo on the prairie, arrived after the treaty signing was complete and after Peter Erasmus had departed. The man who translated Big Bear's words did such a poor job that the resulting misunderstanding set in motion a chain of events that culminated in tragedy for Big Bear and his people. Had Peter been present when Big Bear arrived, the course of history may have turned out differently.

A Long, Long Life
The latter half of Peter's life was more settled, though he had a mixed bag of jobs and employers. Morris hired Peter to perform translation and other duties. Peter was posted to the Cree reserve at Saddle Lake, some distance from his home on the Pakan reserve at Whitefish Lake. There was no place for Peter's wife and family to live at Saddle Lake and he saw them infrequently. Tragically one winter, Peter received word that Charlotte was very ill. In his own memoirs, Peter says he arrived home just in time to say farewell to his dear wife, who died within

a day of his return. In fact, records show that Charlotte passed away a week before Peter's arrival. He remarried in 1882 and had three more children with his second wife, Mary — who also died young, in 1891.

After the Riel Rebellion, Peter left Whitefish Lake, selling his cabin and ten acres of land to the federal government. He may have been forced into this action. All his savings had been deposited in a bank that failed, leaving him destitute. Luckily, he had a job and continued working for the federal department of Indian Affairs. He moved east of Edmonton to the settlement of Victoria. His cabin has since been relocated to Fort Edmonton Park, a "living museum" and historical site in Edmonton.

Peter travelled back to Whitefish Lake to teach at the reserve's school. He remained there until 1909, when he set out to Gleichen, east of Calgary. He stayed there for three years, then more or less retired at the age of 79. He lived with several of his children, moving from household to household, eventually finding his way back to Whitefish Lake. He died on May 28, 1931, at the age of 97.

Chapter 5
Crowfoot
(Isapo-Muxiha)

Of all the First Nations leaders during the turbulent, changing times in the North West, perhaps none were more powerful than Crowfoot, a fierce warrior who earned a reputation for keeping the peace.

Despite receiving many wounds and injuries during his years as a warrior, Crowfoot was tall and lithe with a distinguished, narrow face. Throughout his life, he remained thin and was frequently susceptible to illness, though he never contracted smallpox. By nature, he was generous, always making sure the poor, elderly, or sick people in his band had food and shelter. But even Crowfoot, the mighty warrior and fearless leader, fell victim to the allure of whisky. A man with a hair-trigger temper, when he drank Crowfoot could be downright explosive.

In his youth, he did not join any of the young men's warrior societies, nor was he especially spiritual. However, he did keep items of special significance — a pair of leggings made from the skin of a buffalo calf, and an owl's head. Crowfoot wore the tiny, shrivelled skull woven into his hair throughout his life.

He proved to be an effective leader. His opinions had strong influence and were more forceful than the Blackfoot inclination to fight. He preferred to focus his life on the real suffering of the Blackfoot nation. He never missed a chance to try and help the needy or to speak out for better conditions. For this, he became known as Manistokos or "Father of His People."

Shot Close Takes a New Name

Crowfoot was initially named Astohkomi (Shot Close), when he was born into the Blood nation of southern Alberta, about 1830. He was the first son born to his mother, Attacked Toward Home, and his father, Packs a Knife.

When Shot Close was about two years old, his father was killed during a raid against an enemy Crow band in northern Montana. Attacked Toward Home returned to

Crowfoot

her father's lodge and lived there for three years. One day, some Blackfoot men rode into camp and stayed as guests for several days. One of these men, Many Names, decided to take Attacked Toward Home as his wife.

Many Names wanted to take his new wife north to live among his own people. Attacked Toward Home chose to leave her son in the Blood camp and in the care of his grandfather. However, when it came time to leave, the child ran after his departing mother and would not be left behind. So Many Names generously agreed to take the entire family. To mark the new phase of his life, Shot Close was given a new name by his stepfather: Bear Ghost.

Blackfoot stories say that Bear Ghost was a fierce warrior. He participated in 19 raids, including a journey south to raid the Crows. In the Crow camp was a decorated tipi. The Blackfoot warriors realized the tipi bore sacred markings familiar to them. It had been stolen from a related Peigan band. Bear Ghost was determined to ride boldly into the Crow camp and somehow reclaim the stolen lodge. In his single-minded sprint toward the painted tipi, he was shot in the arm. Even so, he was still the first Blackfoot fighter to reach the sacred lodge. He struck the lodge, symbolically claiming the painted patterns as his own.

To mark the significance of his achievement, Bear Ghost chose to call himself after a legendary Blackfoot warrior, Isapo-Muxiha or Crow Indian's Big Foot. Many years later, when the mounted police came to Blackfoot lands, scout and interpreter Jerry Potts introduced

Isapo-Muxiha as "Crowfoot," a shortened version of his true name.

Crowfoot Takes A New Son

Through his many battles, Crowfoot became known as a fearless warrior. Through raids, trading, and breeding, he acquired a large herd of some 400 horses, a sign of great wealth in Blackfoot society. By the age of 20, his fighting days were behind him. He married Cutting Woman and started a family. He needed his wealth to support his family, which soon included two more wives. He also hired his brother, Iron Shield, and several other men to tend his horses and help him hunt. He needed enough meat to support this large household.

Due to his wealth, his reputation as a warrior, and his astute leadership, Crowfoot became a chief in 1865 upon the death of Three Suns, former leader of the large band to which Crowfoot belonged. Crowfoot's band became known as the Big Pipes.

Although he had adopted the quiet life of a family man and band leader, Crowfoot's campaign as a warrior wasn't finished. On December 4, 1865, Crowfoot and the Big Pipes band were camped a few kilometres downstream from another Blackfoot band. In the middle of the night, the tiny neighbouring camp — which included missionary Father Albert Lacombe — was attacked by a group of Cree and Assiniboine. The Blackfoot were outnumbered at least seven to one but somehow managed to hold off their attackers.

Crowfoot and his band were close enough to hear shots in the night but far enough away that the Cree hadn't noticed the Big Pipes' camp. Under cover of darkness, Crowfoot led his young warriors into the fight. According to Father Lacombe, Crowfoot "fought like a bear." The Cree were driven out of the Blackfoot camp. They hid nearby but with the coming of morning, despite a dense fog, the Blackfoot succeeded in chasing the remaining raiders away.

After a few weeks, Blackfoot bands congregated for the annual Sun Dance — and once again, Crowfoot distinguished himself with an act of incredible bravery. A group of women were picking berries when they encountered a grizzly bear. The women scattered, but a young boy who was with them, tried to defend the women by shooting arrows at the bear. The enraged bear knocked the young man to the ground and began mauling him. On hearing the women's screams, Crowfoot and several other men mounted and rode to the scene, firing their guns. The bear left his bloody victim and ran into the bush.

Crowfoot told the men to ride to the other side of the thicket and attract the bear's attention. Meanwhile,

Crowfoot rode stealthily into the bushes, sneaking up behind the bear. As the bear charged out of the bush toward the other warriors, Crowfoot galloped up to it and plunged his spear into the animal. His horse was terrified and tried to veer away, so Crowfoot leapt from the animal's back and continued his attack on the bear. Finally, in full view of the assembled Blackfoot, Crowfoot killed the grizzly.

In 1873, Crowfoot led his people to the Three Hills area of east-central Alberta. The nearby Cree territory presented an irresistible lure to the young men of his band, including Crowfoot's own son. Though Crowfoot no longer participated in war parties, he saw nothing wrong with his young warriors' desire to find and raid a Cree camp. But one foray proved disastrous, when a small Blackfoot war party was discovered. Crowfoot's son died in the attack. Bent on revenge, Crowfoot and several fighters rode out and found a small Cree camp. The chief killed one Cree man, satisfying his need to avenge his son's death.

Because tragedy had come to his own household, Crowfoot realized the wastefulness of constant warring between the Blackfoot and Cree. He persuaded some of the Cree leaders that a truce should be called. Though fragile, the peace lasted long enough for Crowfoot to actually visit a Cree camp, where he was confronted by a strange coincidence that would forever change his life. His wife had spotted a young Cree man, who looked identical to the son she just lost in war. Crowfoot too was astounded by the physical likeness. The young Cree was Poundmaker.

Crowfoot wanted to know more about this startling young stranger and invited Poundmaker to accompany him and his wife back to the Blackfoot camp. Much to the chagrin of Crowfoot's own young warriors, Poundmaker became part of Crowfoot's household and the chief's adopted son.

Treaty Seven

In the late 1860s and early 1870s, whisky posts throughout Blackfoot territory enjoyed a booming business. For their part, the Blackfoot seemed unable to resist the temptation. They would sell themselves and their families into poverty to obtain the liquor. Fights and murders increased. Even Crowfoot partook in a number of violent incidents fuelled by alcohol. Finally, in 1874, the Blackfoot learned a troop of red-coated policemen from the East were en route to chase away the whisky traders and bring law to the West. Crowfoot greeted this news with relief and gladness.

The NWMP established a fort in the heart of Blackfoot lands, along the Oldman River. On December

1, 1874, Crowfoot went to the post to meet its commanding officer, Colonel James Macleod. He wanted to see for himself what these strangers in his midst were really up to. He was impressed with Macleod, and after witnessing several trials, Crowfoot was convinced the police were as good as their word — that they would treat every man equally before the law.

Although the NWMP did curtail the whisky trade, by this time, the buffalo herds were diminished. Crowfoot's whisky-ravaged people had sunk into starvation and poverty. The chief was deeply troubled about the future. He said, "We all see that the day is coming when the buffalo will all be killed, and we shall have nothing more to live on. Then you will come into our camp and see the poor Blackfoot starving." Then Crowfoot learned from missionary George McDougall that other First Nations to the east were signing treaties with the Dominion government. These treaties, McDougall explained, set aside reserve lands, yet respected the rights of First Nations to continue their traditional ways. Desperate for some reassurance about his people's welfare, Crowfoot welcomed this somewhat erroneous explanation. If this was indeed true, a treaty could not come soon enough.

The Blackfoot treaty — Treaty Seven — was the last treaty to be signed between the Dominion government of Canada and First Nations of the West. September 17, 1887 was the date. Colonel Macleod and Lieutenant-Governor David Laird would speak for the Crown. Crowfoot and the other chiefs of the Blackfoot, Sarcee, Peigan, and Blood nations would speak for the Blackfoot Confederacy. Jerry Potts would perform as translator.

The meeting was to be held at Fort Macleod, but Crowfoot was unhappy with this location. In fact, he refused to come. To avoid a standoff, Macleod hastily agreed to move the treaty meeting to Blackfoot Crossing on the Bow River. This decision angered the Blood and Peigan nation chiefs, who felt they had just as much authority as Crowfoot. But Macleod stood firm — so the Blood and Peigan refused to move north to the new meeting place. Another standoff! It seemed everyone's nose was out of joint and the success of the treaty was in jeopardy. Crowfoot alone was satisfied. At his word, bands of Blackfoot gathered at Blackfoot Crossing, while the Blood and Peigan were nowhere to be seen. Laird issued word that negotiations would be delayed in hopes that the leader of the Blood nation, Red Crow, would arrive.

At last, he could wait no longer. Laird began the discussions by saying, "In a very few years, the buffalo will probably be all destroyed, and for this reason the

Queen wishes to help you to live in the future in some other way. She wishes you to allow her white children to come and live on your land and raise cattle, and should you agree to this she will assist you to raise cattle and grain, and thus give you the means of living when the buffalo are no more. She will also pay you and your children money every year, which you can spend as you please."

Such was the government's offer. Some of the Blackfoot chiefs were resigned, others were angry. For his part, Crowfoot was undecided. He was opposed to signing away his people's traditional life of freedom until the buffalo were well and truly gone. But by then, would it be too late? How long might it take for the Blackfoot to adopt new ways, to learn to support themselves by farming? Crowfoot said he would wait until Red Crow arrived before he made up his mind. At last, Red Crow and his followers came to the meeting. Between them, Red Crow and Crowfoot controlled the fate of some 5000 people. The two chiefs were tied by kinship and marriage (one of Crowfoot's wives was Red Crow's sister). They wished to speak as one voice. The two men and their councils talked on and on. Laird grew impatient.

On September 21, Laird demanded a decision. Would the Blackfoot sign or not? Crowfoot spoke. "If the police had not come to the country, where would we all be now? Bad men and whisky were killing us so fast that very few of us would have been left today. The police have protected us as the feathers of the bird protect it from the frosts of winter. I wish them all good, and trust that all our hearts will increase in goodness from this time forward. I am satisfied. I will sign."

On September 22, 1877, Crowfoot and the rest of the Blackfoot chiefs signed the treaty. Crowfoot placed his trust in the NWMP and the government. Both would prove unworthy of the Blackfoot leader's faith.

The Long Journey
The winter of 1877–78 saw the beginning of extreme hunger, which would plague the Blackfoot for many years. In that dry winter, when prairie fires kept the buffalo far to the south, Crowfoot was forced to make a terrible choice: stay in the territory he knew and loved, or lead his people on a journey to find food.

He guided nearly 2000 Blackfoot east to the Sand Hills in west-central Saskatchewan. Large Cree and Assiniboine camps lay to the south. There was an uneasy truce among these traditional enemies, but all were starving and had no energy to waste on raids. Though there were some buffalo in the area, there was not enough meat to go around. By the spring of 1879,

Crowfoot and his people were destitute. In the search for buffalo, he led them south across the Medicine Line, into Montana. Here they stayed, desperate and unwanted, for two years.

In Montana, the Blackfoot fared little better than they did at home. Buffalo were scarce even here, and the social fabric of the Blackfoot camps began to fray. Crowfoot had trouble controlling his restless young warriors, especially when Cree raiders — the Cree were also in Montana looking for buffalo — boldly stole some of Crowfoot's horses. He refused to allow his young men to raid the Cree and get the horses back. Then one night, another Cree raiding party came to the camp. A boy who was guarding the Blackfoot horses spotted them and quickly raced to Crowfoot's lodge. To the astonishment of his fighters, Crowfoot told them to put down their arms. Then he mounted a horse and rode alone into the night. He called out to the Cree, telling them they must not make war. He invited the Cree to be guests in his lodge, which they accepted, albeit with some trepidation.

Still the Blackfoot could not find enough buffalo. In the spring of 1881, poor and hungry, Crowfoot broke camp and began the weary journey home, more than 600 kilometres away. With no horses to carry them and their possessions, the people walked. Through all weather, dressed in rags, they limped across the prairie in a long, beaten line. After six weeks, those who survived this terrible ordeal arrived at Fort Macleod. After resting for a time, Crowfoot continued to the Bow River and to the rolling hills east of Calgary, where he wanted to set his reserve. Of the 2000 people who had gone to Montana, nearly half had perished by the time Crowfoot brought his people home.

Agitation

Although he was doing everything he said he would by signing Treaty Seven, Crowfoot became increasingly disillusioned. He took a reserve. He and his followers learned to farm, to build cabins. They had forsaken their old ways — buffalo hunting, raiding their enemies the Cree, stealing horses. Yet the government was not holding up its side of the bargain. The Blackfoot were starving. As anger and resentment grew, Crowfoot was frequently called upon to keep things from escalating. Time and again, Crowfoot counselled peace. But he needed all his powers of persuasion and influence.

In January 1882, a Blackfoot man named Bull Elk was swindled out of a cow's head he purchased at the ration house on the reserve. In retaliation, Bull Elk fired his rifle at the ration house employee, who promptly complained to the police. Two NWMP officers arrived on the scene and tried to arrest Bull Elk, but a mob of angry Blackfoot surrounded the redcoats and forced them to surrender him. Then Crowfoot stepped into the fray and upbraided the policemen for trying to arrest an innocent man. He told them he would bring Bull Elk to them for a fair trial. The officers retreated and the situation was defused, but not for long. The officers sent word to Fort Macleod that they needed reinforcements. Twenty men, under Superintendent Crozier, quickly arrived.

Crozier arrested Bull Elk for a second time, inciting fury among the Blackfoot — including Crowfoot, who thought that his promise to bring Bull Elk to the police for a hearing was sufficient. With a hundred warriors, Crowfoot rode to the police cabin to demand Bull Elk's freedom. The police leader and the Blackfoot chief faced one another, pride and anger burning in their eyes. Crozier refused to give up the prisoner, even though he was outnumbered five to one. It was Crowfoot who wisely assessed the situation and backed down. His people had more important concerns than a show of force against the mounted police.

Things settled down for a time. The Blackfoot planted crops in the spring and harvested potatoes, turnips, and wheat in the fall. But disease returned to the Blackfoot in 1883. Crowfoot himself took ill. To make matters worse, the Canadian Pacific Railway was being constructed across the plains. In the summer of 1883, the line reached the banks of the Bow River and the Blackfoot reserve. Crowfoot believed the sickness was caused by smoke from the locomotives and threatened to have his people tear up the tracks. Luckily, Crowfoot's health improved and the situation was diffused.

The year 1883 was an economic disaster for the government of Canada. Costs had to be cut across the board and the department of Indian Affairs was no exception. Staff were dismissed; rations were cut. It was all becoming too much to bear, even for the patient Crowfoot. By the spring of 1884, the Blackfoot leader was willing to listen to the whispers of a Métis rebellion. And the man who had Crowfoot's ear was a Métis messenger from Riel himself: Bear's Head.

Bear's Head had come to Canada from Montana, and Crowfoot made him welcome. The two men spent many hours in conversation. The young warriors were also interested in what the Métis had to say. The reserve's farm instructor became so alarmed at the warriors' mood that he rode to Calgary and reported the goings-on to Inspector Sam Steele, who was in charge of the NWMP detachment. Steele dispatched two constables to arrest Bear's Head. This they accomplished, though not without arousing considerable anger on the reserve. As they were taking the prisoner back to Calgary (a distance of about 80 kilometres) Bear's Head leapt from the moving train and ran off.

Steele decided to ride out and arrest the fugitive himself. Taking two officers and a wagon, he set off eastward to the Blackfoot reserve. The police arrived in the midst of the annual Sun Dance. In a surly mood, hundreds of armed Blackfoot warriors surrounded Steele, who ignored them and boldly stepped into Crowfoot's tipi, where he found Bear's Head.

This was the last straw for Crowfoot. He had been forced to back down when he confronted Crozier. This time, the police had impudently barged right into his lodge. He was deeply insulted and shook with rage. He denied Steele's request to hand over the Métis. Crowfoot stood and advanced toward Steele, who remained rooted to the spot, hand hovering over the butt of his pistol. Steele gave Crowfoot a warning. The Blackfoot leader's better judgment prevailed. He paused, giving Steele just enough time to grab Bear's Head by the collar and haul him outside. A horde of Blackfoot fighters jostled Steele, but he told the two constables to tie Bear's Head to the wagon and prepare to depart for Calgary.

Crowfoot stepped out of his lodge. Steele lectured him about interfering with the police and promised that Bear's Head would get a fair trial. He invited Crowfoot to come to the trial, ensuring the Métis would be revealed as a lair and troublemaker. Steele then wrote a note to the CPR ticket agent at Gleichen — the nearest stop to the Blackfoot reserve — requesting a free ticket for Crowfoot. Once again, the Blackfoot leader backed down, allowing Steele and his men to leave.

Crowfoot made use of his free ticket and rode the train to Calgary to hear the trial. Steele was not there and the evidence against Bear's Head was so weak that the magistrate dismissed the charges. This time, Bear's Head did not return to the Blackfoot reserve — but the damage had been done. His appealing vision of a Métis uprising and a bold new order in the West were fuelling the dreams and aspirations of the Blackfoot warriors — and maybe their leader as well.

War or Peace?
It seemed that all paths were leading to a Native uprising. The settlers were worried. Police and politicians were equally concerned, but Edgar Dewdney had a plan.

Dewdney succeeded David Laird as lieutenant-governor of the North West Territories. In the summer of 1884, he organized a tour for Blackfoot nation chiefs. Crowfoot, his foster brother, Three Bulls, Red Crow of the Blood nation, and Eagle Tail of the Peigan were scheduled to journey to Regina and Winnipeg. Dewdney's motive: to show the Blackfoot leaders how large and powerful the government was and how numerous the non-Native population was. Ultimately, Dewdney wanted the chiefs to decide for themselves that any uprising would be futile.

The great leaders of the Blackfoot Confederacy were escorted, by train, to Regina. Only two years old, Regina was capital of the North West Territories, but the chiefs were unimpressed with the small town. The tour continued to the thriving city of Winnipeg, home to over 20,000 people. Crowfoot returned to his band, more convinced than ever, that the old ways were finished. A new order would push aside the Native traditional life. So when the government further cut the Blackfoot's rations, giving them bacon instead of beef, Crowfoot simply told his people to be patient and work hard on their farming. There was no recourse, even though the government was breaking one promise after another.

Meanwhile, Louis Riel had been spirited back into Canada. In the spring of 1885, news reached the Blackfoot reserve that Riel and his Métis followers were in armed revolt. Métis messengers arrived, imploring Crowfoot to send as many fighters as he could to join the glorious campaign. With heavy heart, Crowfoot swallowed the bitterness of broken promises and smashed hopes. He would not join the fight. But he had one trick left up his sleeve.

Crowfoot had long since made up his mind that fighting would only lead to disaster for the Blackfoot nation. He didn't tell anyone of his decision. He welcomed emissaries from the Métis and Cree, who begged for help in their struggle. He even sent tobacco to Red Crow and Eagle Tail, as a sign that he wanted their support for a war. Perhaps the other two chiefs saw through Crowfoot's joke, or perhaps they realized that the Blackfoot could not win a war against the Canadian government. Either way, the tobacco offering was returned.

Still, Crowfoot bided his time. Rumours that the Blackfoot were about to take up arms put the citizens of Calgary into a frenzy. By March 27, the town's men prepared to defend their settlement and sent their wives and families away by train. The well-known Catholic missionary, Father Albert Lacombe, was sent to the Blackfoot reserve to confer with Crowfoot. The joke had come to an end. On March 30, Lacombe sent a telegram to Prime Minister Macdonald, assuring him that Crowfoot — and therefore the entire Blackfoot nation — would not join the rebellion.

Manistokos, Father of His People
The rebellion passed, but many tragedies were about to befall Crowfoot.

His young daughter became sick and died in the

spring of 1885. Crowfoot was also ill that summer. The following spring, another child died. But then, good news: Poundmaker was freed from prison. It was a happy day when Crowfoot's adopted son stepped into his lodge for a long visit. The two men passed many hours talking, feasting, and smoking, but Crowfoot's joy turned to the blackest of heartaches as he watched his son die before his eyes on July 4, 1886.

Just three weeks after Poundmaker's death, Crowfoot received two important visitors: Prime Minister Sir John A. and Lady Agnes Macdonald. Macdonald wanted a first-hand look at the far North West Territories. On July 22, the prime minister and his wife stepped from the train to be greeted by members of the Blackfoot nation, including Crowfoot. At odds with the importance of the occasion, Crowfoot was dressed in rags, a symbol of mourning for Poundmaker. He also tried to make a point with the prime minister, drawing attention to the terrible state of poverty and suffering on the Blackfoot reserve. Macdonald invited Crowfoot and the other chiefs to express any concerns they might have. Crowfoot made it plain that he expected the government to help his people in return for his neutrality during the Riel Rebellion. Without making any commitments, Macdonald agreed that something should be done. He got back on the train and chugged away.

In late summer, Crowfoot received a communication from Sir John A. MacDonald. This time, it was Crowfoot who would travel. The prime minister had invited several chiefs of the Blackfoot Confederacy to attend a ceremony in Ontario — the dedication of a statue of Mohawk leader, Joseph Brant. A little junket by train! Was this to be the great reward for Blackfoot loyalty?

On September 25, 1886, Crowfoot, Three Bulls, and an interpreter boarded a CPR passenger train and began their eastward journey across the plains to Winnipeg and beyond. On September 30, the Blackfoot chiefs disembarked in Ottawa, where they were treated like royalty and followed about by throngs of people. They continued to Montreal for a number of engagements and events. By October 9, when they returned to Ottawa, Crowfoot was exhausted. He rallied long enough to visit Macdonald at the prime minister's official residence. Once again, Crowfoot turned his attention to the plight of his people. A few days later, too tired and ill to finish the tour, Crowfoot started his homeward journey, accompanied by Three Bulls and Father Lacombe. They arrived back at the Blackfoot reserve on October 20.

His condition worsened with the arrival of cold weather. Crowfoot spent most of that winter confined to his lodge, but the world had not seen the last of him yet.

Crowfoot spent the next three summers visiting his old friends among the Sarcee, Blood, and Peigan. At last, he could travel no more. In his painted lodge, Crowfoot, known with affection as "Father of His People," lay dying. Shamans and medicine men attended him, but their incantations could not rouse the old chief. A doctor was summoned from Calgary, but he could not help either. He prescribed a mustard poultice and a shot of brandy to ease the tightness in Crowfoot's congested lungs. Crowfoot accepted the poultice, but the Blackfoot leader, who had not taken a drink for many years, refused the liquor.

Some time on April 25, 1890, Crowfoot gained enough strength to say these words: "A little while and I will be gone from among you, whither I cannot tell. From nowhere we came, into nowhere we go. What is life? It is as the flash of a firefly in the night. It is as the breath of the buffalo in the winter time. It is as the little shadow that runs across the grass and loses itself in the sunset." Shortly after this speech, Crowfoot fell into a deep sleep. He did not awake.

Chapter 6
Jerry Potts
(Ky-yo-kosi, Bear Child)

Born in Montana, abandoned by his mother, Jerry Potts grew up fast. He was raised by rough men and by his mother's people, the Blood nation. Half-wild as a boy, Jerry learned to be observant, to act first and ask questions later. As an adult, he was short and wiry, slope-shouldered, and with markedly bowed legs from a lifetime on horseback. His keen dark eyes saw everything, but betrayed nothing.

Jerry Potts dressed oddly, even by frontier standards. His pants and jacket were buckskin, leather, or heavy wool in winter. He also wore traditional Blackfoot leggings and moccasins. He was always heavily armed with a handgun, a Winchester rifle, and at least one knife. Soft-spoken and blunt, he seldom expressed any kind of emotion. Above all, he was a man of few words — ironic for someone who made a living as an interpreter and guide.

A Boy With Three Fathers
Jerry's father Andrew Potts immigrated to Pennsylvania from Scotland in the 1830s, searching for a new life. Potts was hired by the American Fur Company and came west to Fort McKenzie in Montana, where he was employed as a clerk and accountant. Popular and well liked, soon Potts was chief factor at the post. He married a Blood woman, Crooked Back. Their son was born in 1840. Potts named his son Jerry, while Crooked Back called the boy Ky-yo-kosi — Bear Child.

Blackfoot, Cree, Crow, Assiniboine, and Gros Ventre peoples visited Fort McKenzie. Young Jerry had a facility for languages. Before long, he could converse with all the people who came to trade with his father. But when Jerry was just a lad, his father was murdered. Crooked Back immediately returned to her family in what is now southern Alberta. Perhaps fearing that the Bloods would not accept her half-Scottish son, she left Jerry behind.

Jerry Potts

A man named Alexander Harvey took the child in. Exactly why he did is a mystery. Harvey was a tough character. Jerry witnessed his first murder at a very young age when Harvey shot a Cree who was apparently intent on stealing horses. Young Bear Child quickly learned to be wary and suspicious.

Though he lived in Fort Benton, Montana, Harvey travelled extensively. He was a hunter, trapper, and trader — and took the boy along on his trips. From early childhood, Jerry learned his way around the open country that is now Montana and southern Alberta. He soon demonstrated his innate ability to recognize landmarks and an unerring sense of direction. He seemed to have a photographic memory for landscapes. At about this time, Jerry had his first taste of alcohol. He developed a strong liking for whisky that would last his entire life.

Eventually Harvey's bad temper and various misdeeds caught up with him. He quietly skipped town, leaving his young charge behind. Jerry next fell in with Andrew Dawson, another Scotsman, who found the lad drunk and decided to take Jerry under his wing. Dawson tried to give Jerry a basic education, though English was never Jerry's strongest language. He spoke in choppy sentences, and he never learned to read or write. Jerry would rather be outdoors hunting and riding, developing his abilities as a marksman, hunter, and tracker.

At age 10, Jerry asked to be allowed to find his mother. Dawson agreed and helped Jerry find the Blood band where his mother lived. She took him in for a few months. He lived among the Blood people, learning the traditions and cultures of the Blood and Blackfoot. Jerry eventually returned to Fort Benton. He accompanied Dawson and other traders on their forays from Fort Benton. Before he was 20, Jerry had travelled much of the Missouri River country, knew the Cypress Hills, had been to the Rocky Mountains, and knew northern Montana and southern Alberta intimately.

When Jerry was in his late teens, Andrew Dawson suffered a severe injury when he fell into a cellar. His health deteriorated, and Dawson decided to return to the eastern U.S. Once again, Jerry Potts was abandoned. But this time, he was a young man and able to fend for himself.

In the early 1860s 23-year-old Jerry was hired by the American Fur Company and sent to Fort Galpin on the Milk River. There was trouble almost immediately. Jerry was drinking one night with a man named Antoine Primeau, who got rougher and more insulting with each sip. Finally, Jerry had had enough of the man's taunting. The argument escalated and Jerry drew his revolver, killing Primeau with a single shot. Jerry was never charged or tried for this killing, but the event had a profound effect on him. He became even more reticent than before, seldom speaking to anyone.

For several years, he divided his time between the Blackfoot, Blood, and Peigan camps, and Fort Benton. When he wasn't working for the American Fur Company, Jerry lived among the Blood and Blackfoot in southern Alberta, near the Oldman and Belly rivers. During these times, he developed a reputation as a fierce warrior and fighter. He defended his family and band against marauding Cree, Assiniboine, Crow, and other enemies. His extensive, encyclopedic knowledge of the vast, open land gave him a distinct advantage over his enemies. He was also a superb rider and shooter. He joined numerous horse-stealing and war parties, earning respect and honour among his mother's people.

Quick As a Cat

One night at Fort Benton after a lengthy drinking spree, Jerry fell into a deep sleep and had a vision that changed his life. Jerry dreamed that his protector spirit was a cat — appropriate for a man who moved with lithe grace, incredible quickness, and amazing stealth. Upon waking, Jerry scoured Fort Benton for a cat. He found a well-fed specimen that belonged to one of the community's prominent citizens. Catching the animal napping, Jerry grabbed, killed, and skinned it. For most of his life, he wore the cat's skin against his own, under his shirt — his guardian spirit. The cat's magic protected him, time and again.

After the killing of Antoine Primeau, Jerry chose to head back to live among the Blood band of his mother's family. It was a long trip from Montana to the Blood camp on the Milk River in Alberta. One day, while leading his packhorse through some dense brush along the Frenchman River, Jerry sensed he was not alone. Suddenly his horse tensed under him. Acting instinctively, Jerry leaned to the side while kicking his horse into a gallop, an action that saved his life. A bullet whizzed through the air where he had been only a second before. Leaping from the saddle, Jerry drew his revolver, but lay motionless on the ground as though wounded or dead. He waited.

Two Cree warriors stepped cautiously from the thicket and approached. When they were at very close range, Jerry suddenly raised his pistol and fired, killing the closest of the two men. The second man tried to load his rifle, but he wasn't fast enough. Jerry stood and fired twice more, killing the man. Then, hearing his horse snort in surprise, Jerry suspected there were other warriors hiding in the brush. He ran for cover and listened intently for several minutes. He concluded that his horse was only responding to the presence of the Cree horses he could not see. He gingerly worked his way through the thick willows until he spotted the two Cree ponies. He captured them both, retrieved his own two horses, and continued his journey.

Some time after this, the Blood followed the buffalo south into Montana. Jerry preferred to hunt alone, so one day he took two good horses and set out in search of bison. He crossed the Missouri and worked his way up a creek with the wind at his back. Suddenly, he was confronted by at least half a dozen armed Crow fighters. Recognizing that the situation called for a cool head and quick thinking, Jerry calmly greeted his enemies — in Blackfoot — and led them to believe he had friendly intentions. He did not let on that he understood every word the Crow men said to one another. They motioned to him that he should follow as they returned to their camp. He nodded. Three Crow warriors led the line of riders from the creek bed with several others saddled behind Jerry.

Jerry listened to the Crows' conversation and learned they were heading toward a large camp. He needed to take swift action, for if the warriors were successful in taking him to their band, he would be, at best, a captive slave; at worst, he would be killed. As the troop rode on, Jerry overheard one Crow persuading the others that they should simply kill him and take his horses.

He heard a rifle being cocked behind him. Once again, he leapt from his saddle just as the shot was fired. The bullet whined harmlessly into the air. With surprise on his side, Jerry was able to fatally shoot all four of the riflemen, and then he turned his attention to the three men who had been riding ahead of him. All he saw was their dust, as they kicked their ponies into a frenzied run.

War With the Cree

The Cree fared better than the Blackfoot when smallpox devastated the plains peoples in 1869–70. As First Nations across the plains counted their losses, the Cree convinced their Assiniboine allies the moment was right to take decisive action against the weakened Blackfoot nation. The Cree gathered their forces. Among the leaders were Big Bear and Piapot, a fiery warrior from the Cypress Hills.

Cree scouts found a small Blood camp, but missed a much larger Peigan camp nearby. On October 24, 1870, under cover of darkness, the Cree and Assiniboine attacked, killing several women and children. The Blood sent runners to obtain help from their allies camped nearby. One messenger went all the way to Fort Benton, where Jerry was enjoying a night of drinking with some friends. Jerry and a companion rode out to help. They

Jerry Potts

met a band of Peigan on the trail and agreed to attack the Cree at dawn.

When he arrived at the beleaguered Blood camp, Jerry noticed a high ridge and sent a number of Peigan and Blood fighters to the top. They rained bullets onto the Cree from this vantage point. After some time, Jerry sensed that the enemy was weakening. The moment had arrived to move, and he led the charge. The Cree ran toward the river and tried to ford it, but the Blood and Peigan fighters overwhelmed them. The battle was a complete rout. It had a devastating effect for the Cree and Assiniboine warriors who had so badly misjudged their foe.

Though Jerry emerged from the battle with no wounds, he was lucky. In the midst of the battle, he came face to face with a Cree fighter who fired at him from point-black range. Jerry threw himself from his horse just as the warrior's gun discharged. Falling to the ground and rolling out of harm's way, Jerry realized there was a ringing in his left ear. He later found it to have powder burns. The warrior's bullet had just missed its mark.

Jerry Potts was a hero of this famous battle and returned to camp with 16 enemy scalps. He had proved himself a fearless fighter and brave leader in battle.

As it turned out, Jerry's name and reputation among the Blackfoot saved the lives of his clients. After this battle took place, Jerry did some guiding in the area. He was leading three men from eastern Canada on a hunting expedition near present-day Pincher

Creek. The day's hunt hadn't turned up any game so by evening Jerry left camp alone and shot a deer. Six or seven Blackfoot were holding his clients at gunpoint upon his return. Jerry approached the young Blackfoot men, talked and laughed with them. The Blackfoot lowered their guns and quietly left. When one of the amazed clients asked Jerry what he'd said to the warriors, in his typical laconic style, he replied, "I told them you're my friends, if they don't leave I'll get mad."

The Redcoats Arrive

Though he had a life-long love for whisky, Jerry could clearly see that alcohol was the downfall of the Native people. He deeply detested what liquor did to the social fabric of the Blackfoot camps. He despised whisky traders, in spite of being a good customer of their illicit trade. His half-brother and mother were both murdered during a drinking spree in their camp — deaths that Jerry avenged by shooting the man responsible, a Blood named Good Young Man.

The Dominion government finally took action to quell the rising violence in the West. The prime minister appointed Colonel George French as the commissioner of a new police force — the North West Mounted Police. French selected some 300 young men from throughout eastern Canada. He trained them in Manitoba and led them westward across the plains in June 1874. The young recruits and their horses faced innumerable hardships as they marched across the prairie. By the time the troops reached the Cypress Hills, they were weary, exhausted — and lost.

En route to establish themselves in the West, the police were looking for the notorious Fort Whoop-up, a trading post established near present-day Lethbridge. In the huge expanse of the western plains, every creek, every coulee, every bluff of cottonwoods looked the same to the new arrivals. Their supplies were running low. Their horses were weary and footsore. Their bright red tunics and shiny riding boots were tattered.

Searching vainly for the whisky fort, the police column finally turned south, heading for the Sweetgrass Hills in Montana. French made camp upon reaching the trees and good grass of the sheltering hills. The men and horses rested while French and his next-in-command, Colonel James Macleod, made their way to Fort Benton to buy supplies and perhaps find a reliable guide. Their first stop was the supply store operated by I. G. Baker, who gladly provisioned them. Then French asked Baker a fateful question: did Baker know of any good guides for hire?

It so happened that Jerry Potts was in town, drinking with his friends at a local saloon. Baker sent his assistant to find him and bring him to the store to meet the redcoats. Jerry was reluctant to leave the bar. Eventually the messenger persuaded Jerry to come and meet the Canadian policemen. He sauntered over to Baker's store to size up them up and find out what they wanted of him.

French wasted no time. He bluntly asked Jerry whether he was interested in a full-time job as a guide and interpreter for the NWMP. French offered a monthly salary of $90 plus food. The deal was struck with a simple handshake and earned Jerry Potts a prominent place in western Canadian history. The date was September 24, 1874.

His new job started immediately. The police had to trust their new guide, as they were completely unfamiliar with the terrain. Jerry led the troops north from the Sweetgrass Hills. No sooner had they started their trek back to Canadian territory, Jerry disappeared and left instructions on which direction the troops should take. The police arrived at the Milk River and found Jerry dressing the carcass of a buffalo he'd killed. Not only did he know how to find his way across the plains, he proved to be an excellent hunter too.

On the way to Fort Whoop-up, Jerry came across the body of a Native man lying in the tall grass. The man had apparently been dead for some time. The body was in an advanced state of decomposition. It was a horrible sight. Macleod asked Jerry what he thought the cause of death might have been. Jerry replied with a single word: "Drunk!"

Finally, after a hard ride of several days, Jerry led the police to the top of a ridge. From this vantage point, they looked down upon Fort Whoop-up and the goal they had so long anticipated. This was why these men came west — to eradicate the whisky trade — and this trading post, hidden in a deep coulee, was the most notorious of all. The men drew their guns and made ready to attack, but Jerry told them to hold their fire and simply ride to the gates of the fort. Macleod and French must have wondered if their guide was setting them up for an ambush. They cautiously followed him as he rode down the slope.

Jerry correctly determined the fort was empty. He and Macleod rode boldly to the gates and banged on them loudly. An old man swung the door open — and invited the troops in for lunch! Hearing of the imminent arrival of the NWMP, the American whisky traders had fled back to Montana, where the long arm of Canadian law couldn't touch them.

The police needed an operations headquarter and shelter from the coming winter. Once again, Macleod turned to Jerry for advice. He recommended a location to the west and led the troops to a spot on the Oldman River. The men set to work, building what would come to be known as Fort Macleod. While they constructed their winter quarters, Jerry rode to various nearby Blackfoot, Blood, and Peigan camps to explain about the new arrivals and why they had come. This simple act of diplomacy paved the way for the NWMP's strong relationship with the Blackfoot nations.

By November, the fort was built. Macleod was ready to receive visits from the Blackfoot chiefs. One by one, Jerry brought many of the chiefs to meet the redcoats and translated for each side — though his style often left both groups wondering exactly what the other had actually said. Being a man of few words, Jerry frequently reduced long, eloquent speeches to the bare essentials. When one prominent leader arrived at Fort Macleod, Jerry even shortened his name from Crow Indian's Big Foot to Crowfoot. He listened carefully to the chief's address, which continued on for some time. When Crowfoot finished speaking, Jerry turned to Macleod and told the officer, "He's damn glad you're here."

Perilous Winter Trips
In February 1875, the NWMP at Fort Macleod learned that whisky traders had set up posts on the Highwood

and Sheep rivers, in the foothills some 300 kilometres to the north. Winter had the entire area in its firm grip. Colonel Macleod sent out a police patrol of 10 men, under Jerry's guidance, to capture the traders and shut down their posts. They left Fort Macleod on February 3. There was trouble immediately. A toboggan broke and three men returned to the fort for a new wagon. The men journeyed about 20 kilometres north and made a frugal camp with no wood for a fire. Instead, they burned buffalo chips and spent a sleepless, shivering night.

The next day was somewhat less frigid and they trekked about 30 kilometres. Although their second camp was more sheltered than the first, a storm roared in during the night and blew their tents apart. The men scrambled for the safety and shelter of the willow thickets nearby and waited out the storm's fury.

Jerry was anxious to get the men moving as he felt the approach of another storm. The party made it to an abandoned whisky post and took shelter. True to Jerry's premonition, a blizzard began to howl around the cabin and the men were forced to remain there for two full days. Though the men were comfortable inside, their horses suffered from the cold, wind, and lack of food. The police set out once more when the storm finally cleared, but the snow was very deep and the horses tired quickly.

Jerry Potts

The party finally reached the Highwood River (shortened by Jerry to High River). They spent the next week rounding up traders, confiscating their goods, and meeting with several Blackfoot bands camped in the area. At last, prisoners in tow, the troop set out on the return journey to Fort Macleod. It was February 19.

The men split into two groups, one guarding the prisoners, the other taking charge of the horses. The wind rose while the snow began to fall. Soon the two groups lost sight of one another. As the storm intensified, the tracks of the leading group were obliterated, forcing the second group to stop where they were, in hopes that Jerry would come find them. They waited for hours, unable to move either forward or back. The wind and snow obscured everything. Some of the men became agitated, fearing they would die in the blizzard. They doubted any man could find his way through such a storm. Just when the situation appeared most hopeless, the men spotted a dim figure barely visible riding toward them. It was Jerry Potts. He led the grateful men to the camp where the lead party was waiting. Three days later, the men returned to Fort Macleod — mission accomplished.

The winter presented a hazard of another kind: the police payroll could not get through. The men at Fort Macleod, including Jerry Potts, had not been paid for some time and there was considerable unrest among the enlisted men. Finally, Colonel Macleod got word from Ottawa that he should ride to Helena, Montana, where he could draw the men's pay from a bank there — a distance of almost 500 kilometres across open prairie, mountains, and hostile Crow country. Macleod immediately called up Jerry. On March 15, five policemen and their guide started the long journey southward.

As they rode toward the Milk River, they encountered some buffalo. Macleod, looking for diversion, made a grave mistake by running his horse after the herd. He singled out an old bull, intending to shoot it. He spurred his horse and ran alongside the snorting buffalo, which suddenly turned and lunged. One of the bull's horns caught Macleod's stirrup and ripped it from the saddle. Macleod almost lost his balance, but managed to stay on his horse. He returned to the group with a sheepish look on his face, and Jerry laconically remarked that he should have spared his horse for the long ride ahead.

The group dismounted for a rest while Macleod fixed his stirrup. Though the day had dawned fine and bright, Jerry noticed a high, thin cloud was advancing from the north. The normally quiet man was suddenly animated and excited, telling the police that a big storm was coming and they had to get going — now. The men hurriedly set out once more and made good time before the snow caught them. The storm quickly turned from a few floating flakes into a howling blizzard. Jerry advised the men to dismount and dig snow shelters in the lee bank of the Milk River. It wasn't an ideal spot as there was no firewood, but it was the best they could do.

The troops took shelter as the wind roared and the temperature dropped. The party stayed in their snow hole for a full day and two long nights. On the morning of the second day, Jerry suggested they move to a new, more sheltered location. It was move or freeze, he pointed out, so the men emerged from their cave. All day, they plodded through deep drifts, the wind tearing at their clothing and whipping the horses' manes and tails. They headed for Rock Coulee, where Jerry knew they could get out of the punishing wind. Finally, as daylight began to wane, they came to a steep downward slope and Jerry instructed them to make another camp. They had arrived at Rock Coulee. Only when the camp was made and the men were in their tents did Jerry reveal that he had become snow blind and could barely see through his swollen, crusted eyes. How he managed to find Rock Coulee was beyond the men's comprehension.

After another miserably cold and sleepless night, the troops set out again. Jerry knew of a U.S. army post on the Marias River. It was their only hope of survival so they headed for the fort. It was another hard day but eventually they arrived and were taken in by the amazed American cavalry. A day's rest was in order, then the police continued to Helena without further trouble. At last, the troops got back to Fort Macleod. Everyone, including Jerry, finally received their pay.

Fort Walsh
Having effectively eradicated the whisky trade in the Fort Macleod region, the NWMP turned their attention east to the Cypress Hills, where American whisky traders were still busy. Macleod decided to send a substantial police contingent east to establish a new fort. James Walsh was to be the commanding officer. In May 1875, he led 160 troops and supply wagons eastward with Jerry Potts as guide and interpreter. Jerry took them straight to a spot with good timber, water, and grass for their horses and the men commenced building their new stronghold, which they called Fort Walsh.

The new NWMP fort was in Assiniboine and Cree territory, traditional enemies of Jerry's people, the Blood. While the police went about their business, Jerry frequently scouted and hunted in the Cypress Hills, alone — a dangerous undertaking. One afternoon, he shot three antelope and was busy dressing the meat. Intent on his task, he let his guard down and five

Assiniboine warriors surprised him. With his rifle lying some distance away on the ground, Jerry appeared to be unarmed and helpless as the fighters surrounded him. The men exchanged insults and threats as Jerry quickly assessed the situation.

Suddenly, he leapt for the cover of an antelope carcass, hiding behind it, and firing his pistol. The Assiniboine warriors fired back, one bullet burning through the sleeve of Jerry's jacket. Jerry's shot grazed one of their horses, which reared and plunged. The rider managed to stay seated but the war party was instantly in disarray and confusion. They turned and galloped away with Jerry firing after them for good measure. He then calmly continued with his work, loading the antelope meat onto his packhorse, and returned to the new fort.

For the balance of 1875 and into the spring of 1876, Jerry divided his time between Fort Macleod, Fort Walsh, and his family among the Blood people. He also continued to drink heavily, going on extended benders between assignments for the police.

Then in November 1876, Macleod heard rumours about a makeshift whisky post in the Fort Walsh area. The wily traders had built their cabin a scant 30 metres north of the Medicine Line so they could scamper to safety in Montana — just a short run away if the police showed up to arrest them. Macleod asked Jerry to scout out the cabin and confirm its exact location without alerting the traders to his presence. Then he should continue to Fort Walsh and lead a contingent of police back to the spot.

Jerry set out alone with a warm Chinook wind for company. He travelled for three days but before he reached the coulee where he suspected the cabin might be, he was overtaken by a sudden winter storm. Alone on the open prairie, with few landmarks to guide him, the famous Jerry Potts was in danger of becoming lost in the blizzard. The storm intensified and the temperature dropped. He kept heading east, hoping to find a creek valley and the shelter of trees. Night fell and still Jerry was on the windswept prairie. He dismounted from his weary horse and walked, leading the animal.

Now in complete darkness, pushing slowly but steadily on with the wind behind him, Jerry suddenly stumbled into a solid object. It turned out to be the box of a sleigh, turned upside-down. He pounded vigorously on the bottom and heard muffled voices from underneath. Without wasting time on formalities, Jerry immediately crawled under the sleigh box where he found a man and boy huddled together under buffalo robes. The man, Tim Holland, was taking his son Harry from their home in Helena, Montana to visit a brother's new homestead on the Red Deer River. When the storm roared in, Holland got lost. Then the sleigh turned over, and his team of horses ran off. Holland was sure he and his son were doomed until he heard Jerry hammering on the sleigh box.

The three huddled together under the robes, sharing Jerry's food. Snow drifted right over their shelter, insulating them from the intense cold, but preventing them from knowing whether it was day or night. Outside, the storm continued. From time to time, Jerry ventured out to look after his two horses, but beyond that, the trio stayed under the sleigh for three full days. At last, the weather cleared, leaving deep drifts and extreme cold.

Now that the storm had passed, Jerry had work to do. He helped Holland dig the sleigh out then resumed his search for the whisky post. After ploughing through deep drifts for several kilometres, he crested a ridge and gazed down upon the cabin, tucked almost out of sight amid the brush in a valley bottom. There were no tracks in the fresh snow around the post so Jerry boldly rode down to see whether anyone was home. All he found was a note from one of the whisky traders to his accomplices. Somehow the trader had been tipped off that the NWMP were going to come looking for him and he'd decamped to Fort Benton.

For Jerry, the discovery couldn't have been better. The cabin was comfortable and well stocked with food, warm blankets, and firewood. He rode back to the Hollands' sleigh and brought the cold, hungry, weary travellers to the whisky post, where the three spent an agreeable night. With the man and boy safe in the whisky cabin, Jerry rode to Fort Walsh and arranged for a rescue party to fetch them — and then burn the cabin.

Treaty Seven and Beyond
The NWMP once again made use of Jerry's knowledge of Blackfoot language and culture when it came time to negotiate and sign a treaty between the Canadian government and the Blackfoot Confederacy. Macleod asked Jerry to visit the many Blackfoot, Blood, and Peigan bands in the area and explain that the government wished to make a treaty with them. Jerry set off, taking tobacco and other gifts to the chiefs.

After more than a year of such travels and discussions, at last the Blackfoot people gathered east of Fort Calgary (at a place called Blackfoot Crossing, so named by Jerry Potts) to meet with the Dominion government representatives. Jerry was the official interpreter. Lieutenant-Governor David Laird stood before the assembled chiefs with Jerry at his side, ready to translate his speech. Laird began his address, using flowery language and political terminology that Jerry had never heard before. Laird kept talking while Jerry stared at him, trying to follow his convoluted oration. At last Laird paused. There was silence. The pause lengthened. Then Jerry spoke. "I don't understand a damn word." So saying, Jerry stomped off angrily, and the assembled police had to find another translator.

Despite this setback, Jerry Potts continued to work for the NWMP for 22 years as a guide, scout, and interpreter. He travelled extensively and served the police at Fort Macleod and Fort Walsh. But when he wasn't scouting or working with the police, Jerry lived among the Blood people in the Porcupine Hills, just northwest of Fort Macleod.

Jerry married four women. His first wife was Mary, a Crow woman 11 years his younger. They had a son, Mitchell, whom Jerry loved dearly. But the marriage did not last. When Jerry moved away from Fort Benton and into Canada, Mary did not want to stray that far from her people so the couple split up. Mary took Mitchell with her, one of the great regrets of Jerry's life.

Jerry Potts was a two-sided coin who led two very different lives. Though he was not a belligerent person — the opposite, in fact, he was quiet and retiring — he seemed to attract fighting and trouble and always wound up in the thick of things, whether it was a

Blackfoot war party or a bar-room brawl. Jerry was fearless and cool-headed under fire, gaining a reputation as a dangerous enemy that lasted his entire lifetime.

As he got older, Jerry turned increasingly to liquor, in part to ease a growing pain in his chest that was either tuberculosis or cancer.

Late in life, Jerry gained a second lucky charm. In the early 1890s, Jerry went duck hunting with a constable from Fort Macleod. They found a marshy spot surrounded by thick, tall cattails — perfect duck habitat. Jerry suggested they split up as they approached the tall vegetation. The constable crept through the bush. Suddenly a fine big duck burst from cover directly in front of him. The policeman shot and felled the duck, but as he lowered his shotgun he saw, to his horror, Jerry lying on the ground, in obvious pain. Rushing over, the constable arrived just as Jerry sat up, his hand on a bloody wound where a single pellet had struck him behind the left ear. The pellet was still there, just under the skin — but when the constable offered to cut it out, Jerry refused. It was the first bullet wound he'd ever had and he was convinced that the pellet was good luck.

Some years later, though, Jerry lost his lucky pellet charm. During his frequent drinking bouts, he repeated the story of his lucky pellet over and over, to the annoyance of everyone who knew him. Finally, a young man who'd heard the story once too often asked to see the wound. Jerry willingly leaned over — and the man whipped out his knife, quickly slicing Jerry's skin, exposing the lucky pellet. As Jerry yelped in surprise, the pellet popped out.

To Jerry, this was a serious blow. With the pellet gone, so was his good luck. His health declined rapidly and his drinking increased. Eventually he was admitted to the infirmary at Fort Macleod. He died on July 14, 1896 at the age of 58.

Jerry Potts is buried at Fort Macleod. Three of his descendants became RCMP officers.

Bibliography

Cameron, William Bleasdell. *Blood Red The Sun*. Edmonton: Hurtig Publishers, 1977 (5th Edition. First published 1926).

Dempsey, Hugh A. *Big Bear: The End of Freedom*. Vancouver, BC: Greystone Books, Douglas & McIntyre, 1984.

Dempsey, Hugh A. *Crowfoot Chief of the Blackfeet*. Halifax, NS: Goodread Biographies, paperback edition, 1988 (First published by University of Oklahoma Press, 1972.)

Dickason, Olive Patricia. *Canada's First Nations: A History of Founding Peoples From Earliest Times*. Toronto, ON: McClelland & Stewart, 1992.

Erasmus, Peter (as told to Henry Thompson). *Buffalo Days and Nights*. Calgary, AB: The Glenbow Institute and Fifth House Publishing, 1999.

Bibliography

Ewers, John C. *The Blackfeet: Raiders on the Northwestern Plains.* Norman, OK, USA: University of Oklahoma Press, 1958.

Fardy, B. D. *Jerry Potts, Paladin of the Plains.* Langley, BC: Mr. Paperback, 1984.

Haig, Bruce. *James Hector, Explorer.* Calgary, AB: Alberta Historical Resources Foundation, Detselig Enterprises Ltd, 1983.

Hollihan, Tony. *Sitting Bull in Canada.* Edmonton, AB: Folklore Publishing, 2001.

Jenish, D'Arcy. *Indian Fall: The Last Great Days of the Plains Cree and the Blackfoot Confederacy.* Toronto, ON: Viking Press, 1999.

Long, Philip S. *Jerry Potts: Scout, Frontiersman and Hero.* Calgary, AB: Bonanza Books, Ltd, 1974.

MacEwan, J. W. Grant. *Portraits From the Plains.* Toronto, ON: McGraw-Hill Company of Canada Ltd, 1971.

Miller, J. R. *Big Bear (Mistahimusqua): A Biography.* Toronto, ON: ECW Press, 1996.

McHugh, Tom. *The Time of the Buffalo.* New York, NY, USA: Alfred A. Knopf, 1972.

Petrone, Penny, Editor. *First People, First Voices.* Toronto, ON: University of Toronto Press, 1983.

Ray, Arthur J. *I Have Lived Here Since the World Began: An Illustrated History of Canada's Native People.* Toronto, ON: Lester Publishing, Key Porter, 1996.

Sluman, Norma. *Poundmaker.* Toronto, ON: The Ryerson Press, 1967.

Spry, Irene M. *The Palliser Expedition: The Dramatic Story of Western Canadian Exploration 1857-1860.* Saskatoon, SK: Fifth House Publishing, 1963, 1995.

Photo Credits

All images are reproduced courtesy of the Glenbow Archives.

Acknowledgments

The author acknowledges the following sources for the quotes contained in this book: the exceptionally detailed and insightful biographies of Big Bear and Crowfoot by Hugh Dempsey; the memoirs of Peter Erasmus, published as the book *Buffalo Days and Nights*, in addition to supporting information about the Palliser Expedition by noted historian Irene Spry; and the thoughtful, sympathetic interpretation of major events in the West as presented by D'Arcy Jenish in his book *Indian Fall: The Last Great Days of the Plains Cree and the Blackfoot Confederacy*. These sources, along with extensive background information from numerous other published materials, have helped me to form a picture of the dedication and courage with which these five remarkable men — Big Bear, Poundmaker, Crowfoot, Peter Erasmus, and Jerry Potts — lived their amazing lives.

AMAZING STORIES™

SAM STEELE

The Wild West Adventures of
Canada's Most Famous Mountie

HISTORY/BIOGRAPHY
by Holly Quan

Sam Steele
ISBN 1-55153-997-7

About the Author

Holly Quan lives in the foothills of southwestern Alberta among the poplars and coyotes. She's the author of Amazing Stories: Sam Steele for Altitude Publishing. She's also written two guide books, in addition to writing magazine articles on travel, food, horses, marketing, and whatever else piques her interest. When she's not busy on her novel manuscript — a work now many years in the making — she loves to ski, ride, hike, swim, drink wine with her friends, and howl at the moon.

OTHER AMAZING STORIES

These titles are available wherever you buy books. If you have trouble finding the book you want, call the Altitude order desk at 1-800-957-6888, e-mail your request to: orderdesk@altitudepublishing.com or visit our Web site at www.amazingstories.ca

New AMAZING STORIES titles are published every month. If you would like more information, e-mail your name and mailing address to: amazingstories@altitudepublishing.com.